WHAT GOD HAS DONE

WHAT GOD HAS DONE

THE STORY OF
THE LATIN AMERICAN
MENNONITE BRETHREN
CONFERENCE

ANNA HIEBERT ESAU

Kindred Press

Winnipeg, MB, Canada   Hillsboro, KS, U.S.A

WHAT GOD HAS DONE

Cover Design by Sleeping Tiger Artworks,
Winnipeg, MB.

Printed in the United States of America by
Multi Business Press,
Hillsboro, Kansas 67063

International Standard Book Number: 0-919797-49-0

FOREWORD

In praise and thanksgiving to God our Savior Jesus Christ, this book has been written for the members, children and friends of the LAMB Conference, and is fondly dedicated to the memory of the missionaries and El Faro teachers who were supported by the Mennonite Brethren of North America. God has used the Southern District to begin this great work of evangelism in South Texas along the Rio Grande.

Special thanks are due to the various members who served on the Mission Board. A good number have gone to their reward, but the work is going on. Thanks are extended to all who in any way provided materials such as reports, answers to questionnaires, pictures and personal reports as well as records of various LAMB Boards.

Special thanks go to Ben H. Wedel who presented the idea of a history to the LAMB Conference in November, 1982. Also special mention must be made of Mrs. Sarah Neufeld, Fresno, California for sending much material and pictures of the early years to aid in accuracy.

Thanks are due Louise and Jonathan Esau, and Linda Haughey for doing the typing.

The Educational Board of LAMB recommends this book to our members, the Mennonite Brethren Conference, and all others interested in the work of missions. We thank God for what He has done in the Rio Grande Valley.

THE EDUCATIONAL BOARD
Mr. Alvin Neufeld — chairman
Mrs. Gregoria N. Guerra — secretary
Miss Maria Palomo — treasurer
Miss Yolanda Villearreal
Mrs. Idalia G. Chapa
Miss Elizabeth Tagle

PREFACE

In the Fall of 1936, the Southern District Mennonite Brethren Conference received a vision and took the most heroic step of faith ever undertaken in its history. The pastors and delegates who attended that Conference at Fairview, Oklahoma were moved by the Holy Spirit and given a zeal and love for the Mexican Americans. They looked at the Rio Grande Valley that many had heard of through P.E. Penner, a Bible expositor. H.W. Lohrenz, then secretary-treasurer of the Board of Foreign Missions, was used of the Lord to warm hearts and stimulate a vision for evangelism among Mexican people. With enthusiasm, this Conference of 1936 accepted Harry and Sarah Neufeld to go and locate a field in the Summer of 1937.

The Conference of the Southern District in 1936 consisted of four large churches, a number of smaller ones, and some struggling to get established, seventeen in all. Yet all stood together to begin a new mission work. From a small beginning, this work in South Texas grew, and was guided and supported by the Southern District. For this reason, the members of the Latin American Mennonite Brethren shall be forever grateful, and thank God for what He has done.

Anna Hiebert Esau

CONTENTS

CHAPTER 1

THE LOWER RIO GRANDE VALLEY OF TEXAS

A. THE RIVER

The Rio Grande is the fifth longest river of North America, 1,800 miles long. It begins in the snow-covered mountains of Colorado and flows south and east, down to form the southern boundary of the state of Texas. "Rio Grande" means "great river" and it truly was, not only long but also a deep and wide stream when explorers found it. Boats came up as far as Rio Grande City and Roma for many years. In Mexico this river is called "Rio Bravo" or "Rio Bravo del Norte." In spring heavy rains and melting snow filled the river to overflowing, thus causing much damage to villages and cities built on its very banks. It was especially destructive after excessive rains caused by hurricanes fell in the Rio Grande watershed. Now Falcon Dam holds the waters back that come from its tributaries as well. This huge earthen dam has the picture of President Eisenhower on it, who came to dedicate it together with officials from Mexico, about 1954. Since then other dams have been built so the lower valley only suffered damage from river water during hurricane Beulah, because the rains fell below the dam. The Rio Grande is the lifeblood of this strip of land along its northern bank, known as the "Lower Valley of Texas." The cities, towns and villages now get their water supply from the river. Water is pumped into purifying plants and from there into tanks on towers and piped to each home and business. Then the river water is held in a network of lakes. From these reservoirs smaller canals lead to fields and groves that keep the valley lush green.

B. THE LOWER RIO GRANDE VALLEY

That strip of land along the tip of Texas, basking under blue skies, is called the "Valley." Coming down U.S. Highway 281, one comes to the city of Edinburg (the county seat of Hidalgo) and finds himself in the midst of the "Magic Valley." This charming, semi-tropical part of Texas is composed of four large counties, Starr at the west, more arid Hidalgo in the center, and Cameron and Willacy along the Gulf of Mexico. It is about 150 miles from Rio Grande City, past Brownsville, to the Gulf of Mexico. It has no mountains, only some river breaks at Rio Grande City and some near the coast of the Gulf of Mexico. It is almost flat, fertile land that slopes gently to the river or to the Gulf of Mexico. The low-lying land near Rio Grande City is only a few miles wide, but downstream it soon widens out 20 to 30 miles north of the river.

Before the Anglo settlers came to this part of Texas, it was a jungle of Mesquite, Texas Ebony, Tepehuaje, Huisache (Sweet Acacia), Rio Ash (Fresno), Retama (Palo Verde), Hackberry (Palo Blanco), one native palm (Sabal or Texas Palmetto) near the mouth of the river, plus many other small and larger trees. Underneath was the underbrush of a great variety of plants such as prickly pear (Nopal) and many other cacti, purple sage (Ceniso), yucca, century plant, Spanish moss and mistletoe growing on Mesquite trees.

In this jungle lived deer, wild hogs (Havelina), bobcats (lynx), coyotes and many smaller animals like the oppossum, raccoon, skunk, snakes, etc. There still are many birds, among them the Green Jay, and the Chachalaca only found here. The white-winged and Turtle Doves are still being hunted each fall.

The settlers cleared the land using Mexican labor and formed an irrigation system to water their fields and groves. Oranges, grapefruits, lemons, tangerines, and avocados were planted on small and larger tracts or ranches. On the rest of the land many vegetables such as carrots, onions, sweet peppers, cabbage, lettuce, beets, tomatoes, green beans, potatoes, etc. grow on small and large fields west toward Rio Grande City on to La Casita Farms and others. Near Rio Grande City many cantaloupes and honeydews are grown and shipped all over the nation. These are harvested the end of May and early June. All over the Valley there are fields of sugar cane and grains such as milo and corn as well as cotton. Two and at times three crops are harvested on a field during a year. The beauty of citrus groves disappears where irrigation ends and the Rio clay begins west of Mission. The city of Mission, however, is the home of Ruby Red grapefruit and has its own Citrus Festival each year. Some miles west of Mission the chaparral (native growth) was left until recent years, which blooms at various times after rains. On these ranches Brahma cattle thrive on the brush. Still further west cattle such as Herefords and other breeds run in herds. These ranchers do not irrigate but depend on rains to keep their pastures green.

To beautify the landscape many species of ornamental dates as well as fruit-bearing ones, fan and cocoa palms with their soft fronds were planted along roads, around fields and near homesteads. McAllen has so many palms it is called "The City of Palms." All over the Valley roses and poinsettias bloom in fall and winter. Oleander and bougainvilleas may bloom all year if frost does not come to destroy them.

To this winter paradise come many people to escape the cold of the north. So groves now taken into growing city limits have trailer spaces between the trees.

There are also alcoholics and drug addicts who drift to the Valley to escape the ice and snow of northern states. They live outside in parks or whatever type of shelter they may find. Stephouse and other agencies are trying to help them to again become useful citizens.

The tip of Texas has its own schools, such as Pan American University and many other educational institutions. Among them is the Rio Grande Bible Institute which trains Spanish workers as well as teaches the Spanish language to missionaries going to Latin American countries. There are churches of nearly every denomination as well as cults found in America. Then it also has its own television stations as well as Christian Spanish and English radio stations. Thus it makes the Valley a little world all of its own. A quote from one Valley resident will illustrate how folks feel about it. "We're not really like the U.S. We're not really like Mexico. We're, well, different. We're the Valley."

This beautiful Valley received a severe blow December 24 and 25, 1983. The awful freeze turned all the citrus brown and piled up the frozen fruit on the ground. Many of the young groves had to be uprooted and the older ones trimmed back to where new growth came out of the large branches. Some groves look nice again though set back a few years.

At first all palms looked dead but in time many came out again, except the more tender cocus were mostly all wiped out and many of the very tall old Washingtonians are also dead. Many tender shade trees and shrubs also are gone. But it was a joy to see some native plants and others such as poinsettias and bananas come out from the roots.

The sugar cane also was frozen but it has come back. Many native trees also are coming back. The freeze did enormous damage and will change the landscape of the Valley. This freeze of 1983 will go down in history as one of the bad ones.

C. THE POPULATION OF THE LOWER RIO GRANDE VALLEY

Long before Texas became a part of the United States, Spain claimed the vast territory north of the Rio Grande. The Spanish were out to conquer lands and souls; Catholic priests followed the Spanish armies, setting up missions to teach native Indians the Spanish language and convert them to the church of Rome.

Spain established Reynosa and Camargo on the south side of the river and gave large land grants to certain families to keep other nations out of this territory.

In Mexico the Indian tribes still hold to their native languages, speak of themselves as the indigenous people and refer to all others who are not pure Spanish as "mestizos," mixed Spanish and Indian, or just mixed tribes who now only speak Spanish. In the Valley there are only a few who still know if their grandfather or grandmother was Spanish or Indian. In the Pharr Church there is a Mrs. Rios who is very fair with brown eyes and soft hair. She says, "They call me 'bolilla'" (nickname used for an Anglo). There are also those who do not have Spanish names, such as "Franz" and "Jones." In Premont there are several Mexican families with Anglo names.

The Hispanics (all people who have their cultural origin either in Spain or Portugal) are seeking for a name that would retain their racial characteristics and yet identify them as U.S. citizens. In California they like to be called "Chicanos," but in the Valley some old folks remember a Mexican rebel gang by that name. The term "Latin" was accepted by Harry Neufeld for his book and is also used by the Mennonite Brethren Conference. Therefore, this work was named LAMB or Latin American Mennonite Brethren. Some members of this conference prefer to be called Mexican Americans.

The Mexican Americans in the Valley, or in any other part of the U.S., are not Spanish nor are they Indian. They have accepted the Spanish language and much of its culture and its religion, but have retained many Indian customs and beliefs. During the past twenty years many of the children of former migrants have come into the mainstream of American life. Many are now in professions and work side by side with the Anglo-Americans.

Due to large families and a continual stream pressing to come into Texas, the Valley population is by far more of Mexican blood than any other. In Rio Grande City there are only a few Anglo-American families. The bulk of Anglos of the Valley live in the citrus belt and in the cities such as Mission, McAllen, Harlingen, Brownsville and Edinburg. There is also a sprinkling of a black population in the Valley.

In winter the population swells with tourists who come to enjoy the mild weather for up to six months. The many trailer parks fill up with Anglos from the northern states and Canada. Every type of sport and recreation is provided. Bibleville, a Christian Bible Conference ground near Alamo, Texas, is in the heart of this Valley. Camp Loma de Vida, nine miles north of Edinburg, is gearing to provide another Christian winter visitors' park.

Politically, the Valley is overwhelmingly Democratic, although a Republican party has recently been established. Texas had a Republican governor, though not elected by the Valley. Years ago the name "Republican" had a derisive connotation.

D. THE SPANISH OF THE MEXICAN AMERICANS IN THE VALLEY

Long ago before the American borders were closed, many landless people crossed the river to find an easier life. They never thought it possible to learn English and become Americans. Unlike people from other countries, who learned English and American ways soon after arrival, the Mexican Americans maintained close contact with their homeland and its language. Their migratory lifestyle also limited their ability to learn English; because they earned a living by following various crop harvests, they frequently had to leave before school had ended, returning long after it had begun. Many people, as a result, never learned to speak English; said one person, a senior citizen born and raised in Hidalgo County, "It used to be so difficult to communicate with the Americans, but now many have learned to speak Spanish."

But what kind of Spanish? Most people simplify the language, mixing English and Spanish together. Some put "el" or "la" before an English noun; sometimes English verbs become Spanish. "Brincar," for example, is Spanish for "to jump," but many use "jumpar" instead.

It is a blessing to know two or more languages if spoken correctly. So something good will come out of the bilingual program in Texas schools. Children will learn to read and write a correct Spanish. There are those who do speak a good Spanish, especially those who came from Mexico as literate adults. They and their children do not speak the colloquial known as "Tex-Mex."

E. THE MEXICAN AMERICAN PEOPLE OF THE VALLEY

Mexican Americans love beauty and like to dress well and furnish their homes as well as possible. Seeing them on the streets you cannot tell what kind of a home they come from. As among other Americans, some pay for what they buy, but others use credit cards and when something goes wrong they are in trouble.

Financially there are some who are wealthy, most of them take care of themselves, while the seasonal unskilled workers cannot support their families, so rely on welfare and food stamps.

The Mexican Americans as a race are described by Harry Neufeld in his book, *Eight Years Among Latin Americans.* He says, "The Mexican people are a race of courteous, kind, gentle, hospitable and open-hearted, sincere people one to another as well as to all who treat them well. There are, of course, some bad ones among them as in any race, but they are by far in the minority. All these years we have lived among them as one of their own people and we could not wish for better neighbors. It would be hard to find a class of people who can outdo them in showing true courtesy and sympathy in spite of all their weaknesses and inabilities to advance socially and educationally." This was written in 1947 and much has changed since that time, some for better and some for worse. There is more crime now than there used to be in the Valley, but less than in the great cities of our land. Cars and trucks are being stolen and with friends from Mexico, transferred across the river. Then there is traffic in drugs, and ring leaders have been arrested and the contraband taken. There also is stabbing and shooting when men are drunk. But these criminals are by far in the minority. But there are cantinas (saloons) in or near every village, town or city.

Harry Neufeld once said, "We have two kinds of Mexicans, one group who wants to learn and better their lot, the other wants to keep things as they are." Those who have applied themselves have learned and are teachers, nurses, doctors, lawyers, merchants, salespersons,

etc. Many young adults, whose grandparents or parents were migrants, now live here as self-supporting citizens.

Harry Neufeld continued, "Nevertheless this must be said, [the
Mexican people] are a suspicious and very cautious race. Many of them
have met with ill treatment by the Anglo-Americans, especially the
older ones in the early days of 'Valley' history. They look with suspi-
cion upon every project and advancement which Anglo-Americans put
forth which involves them, whether it is for their good or not." Even
if much has changed, there still is a barrier between the races, though
this is broken down among believers. One Mexican sister, a member
of Mennonite Brethren, while embracing Anna Esau said, "I love you
just as I do my own people," and she meant it. This is true of other
believers as well. They do anything to aid those who once brought the
gospel light to them.

At Premont, Anna Esau was called "gringa" by a smiling little
girl because she knew no other name for people who are not of her race.
In the Valley "bolillo" (a small loaf of white bread) is probably used
more than "gringo."

The Mexican people are not dirty nor are their homes dirty. Even
the most humble huts are usually tidy. Anna Esau says, "I know
of only a few families of the many I have learned to know, who were
careless in their housekeeping."

The Mexican American people have a culture all of their own.
They attend movies and musicals and produce music of their own,
though not much is related to their church. They have their own musi-
cians who sing and play the old ranchero music as well as the new
various kinds of rock on radio and television. There is much dancing
at their parties, also drinking. The believers and young people of the
LAMB churches still love to sing gospel songs and choruses. There are
persons who naturally have wonderful voices and they sing with all
their heart.

F. PRACTICES AND BELIEFS OF MEXICAN AMERICANS

The church of Rome is very rigid in its doctrine and at the same
time very flexible. It permits members to believe most anything as
long as they are baptized, confess and practice the rules of the church.
Because of this the church in Mexico and here in the Valley is very
different than it is in the northern states or in Canada.

One more or less harmless practice is to send someone a gift. If
the recipient is grateful, he or she is expected to return something on
the same plate or whatever it came in. For example, a neighbor of the
Esaus' in Premont began to bring some clabbered milk in a milk buck-
et. Each day there was a little more clabbered milk. At last the boy,
who could not understand why these "gringos" could not know what
he wanted, longingly looked at the cornfield in the garden. It dawned
on Anna Esau, "Now I know what he wants." So she emptied the pail,
washed it, and went to the garden and filled it with corn ears. The boy

eagerly took it and never again brought any more clabbered milk. The Esaus rather gave the corn than have him help himself.

Another practice strange to Anglo-Americans is helping to provide many of the things needed in a wedding. It is an unwritten law that if one honors you by asking you to do or give something, if at all possible, you do not refuse. Thus, shortly before her wedding, the bride chooses her "padrinos" (godparents) to provide the necessities for a pretty wedding procession. Weddings are different among Mexicans than among Anglos. Weddings may be elaborate with a large number of "padrinos" (couples) marching in the procession. Each one of these buys the gift needed in the wedding.

Some carry the objects such as the cushion on which the couple kneels. One pair carries the "Lazo" (lasso) used to put over both bride and groom to signify union. Another brings the treasure chest with ten coins, dimes, quarters or dollars as they are able, to indicate the pair is not to be in want. At evangelical weddings, one carries a white Bible. Others, who furnished the cake, the knife to cut it, the decorations in the chapel and in the social hall, just march. Thus the wedding absorbs many of the gifts that the couple gets. The groom provides the wedding dress of the bride.

Then there is the belief that if you think someone or something is beautiful you must touch it or you give it the "evil eye." The Harry Neufelds learned about "mal ojo" when their cow became sick. One of the brethren wisely instructed the missionary what was the matter with the cow. "Why do you think so?" asked Harry Neufeld. "Because she has 'mal ojo'," replied the brother. "What is that?" questioned the missionary. "Well," said the brother, "that means that if somebody likes a certain thing or a person and does not touch it or him, something terrible will happen. Your cow was much admired by our uncle who often said, 'I must go over and touch her or something might happen to their cow.' Since he had not done that, the cow was sick."

The missionary told the young believer that Christians do not believe such things. "But it is true, we have seen that too many times," said the young man. "No, dear brother, that is not true," answered Harry Neufeld. "The cow did not die but got well. We prayed and trusted in Jesus. So Jesus was the power. So don't believe that about 'mal ojo' any more. It is not true."

Just how deep-seated this belief is, the following story will show. In another mission one Sunday evening Elisa, who had been in Sunday School ten years, came to church very excited. She asked, "Where is Lucy?" "She is not here, so must be at home," answered the missionary. "No, she is not there, and we need her just now," was the anxious reply. "Why do you need Lucy just now?" "Well, she was at our house this afternoon and said 'Rosie was a cute girl,' but she never touched her. Now she is very sick vomiting." The missionary prayed silently, "Lord, don't let them find Lucy. Rosie just has an upset stomach; it will go over." They did not find Lucy, and Rosie was well in a short time. That family had an opportunity to see that touching, or not doing so, had not made Rosie sick nor well.

Another thing among the people that is foreign to the missionary is the belief in "susto." The following experience is adapted from Harry Neufeld's book. Harry was called to take a twelve-year-old girl to the doctor, who found she had malta fever. Medicine was prescribed and suggestions were given to bring about a cure. However, the doctor said that it would take a long time before she would be entirely well.

After a week or two of treatment, the child was not improving very much and the mother, being anxious, easily fell into the temptation of old beliefs and age-old remedies of a primitive people. Therefore, one day when Harry Neufeld made his rounds to this home to visit the patient, the mother met him with a peculiar smile and twinkle in her eye and said in Spanish, "Now we know what is the matter with our daughter." "Is that so?" asked the missionary rather surprised, "and what might that be?"

"Well," the mother said, "she has 'susto'."

"'Susto', what is that?" asked Harry Neufeld.

"Don't you know what 'susto' is?" she asked in astonishment.

Harry returned home two miles away, got a dictionary and found the word "susto" means "fear." He then drove back to the sick child's home and announced, "Now I know what 'susto' means."

"But why do you think that the child has 'susto'?" he inquired.

"Well I know because a lady came here and said so," was her quick and triumphant reply.

"When?"

"Yesterday."

"Who was the lady?"

"I don't know that."

"Have you ever seen her before?" Harry questioned her.

"No, I have not."

"Well, how does the lady know that she has 'susto'?", he asked.

"Well," and with the typical shrug of the shoulders and protruding the lower lip of her mouth she answered, "I don't know."

"And are you willing to believe what she said?"

"Y-e-s," doubtfully came her reply.

"And you are willing to trust a perfectly strange lady whom you don't know and don't know where she came from? Are you going to believe her more than you believe me, a man who is with you every day? Furthermore, are you more willing to believe her than a competent doctor who has tested the child's blood and knows what her sickness is?"

She shrugged her shoulders and with a weak response said, "Well, I don't know."

He continued, "And after the girl has been taken to the doctor and I spent money for the medicine, for gas and oil on the car to take her there, and have been kind enough to help you every day? Are you going to disregard all that and believe a perfectly strange woman who says she has 'susto'? Let me ask your daughter a few questions."

"Lupita, have you ever been afraid of anything?"

"No," came the quick reply.

"Did you ever get scared?"

"No," she responded clearly.

"Are you afraid now?"

"No," she answered again.

"When did you get this 'susto' that your mother talks about?"

"I don't have any 'susto'," was her affirmative reply.

"You see, mother, your own child says she does not have it. Don't you think you ought to believe me or the doctor more than this stranger whom you have never seen before?"

"Well, I guess so," came the halted answer.

"Then I am going to ask of you this favor. When that strange woman comes here to cure your daughter, don't you let her touch her. Keep her out of the house. God will hear our prayers and she will get well."

God did answer and Lupita became a Sunday School teacher. Harry Neufeld adds, "but see how these people are chained by false beliefs and superstitions."

Not all Mexican Americans believe in the many superstitions but many, especially the illiterate, do still go to curanderos (healers). Some of them use herbs and are called the good ones, whereas others practice witchcraft. It is believed "susto" is a sickness when the heart is frightened after some upsetting experience. The patient is urged to remember what has happened to bring on the spell. If he can't remember, he is taken to a curandero. He checks the pulse. If it is weak and slow and then races fast, it is pronounced "susto." To cure the patient he is taken to a priest to be blessed with holy water.

Some families do not go to curanderos but have their own cure called "sweeping." The child or adult is placed on the floor and covered with a sheet or a red cloth. Grandma then takes a broom and begins to sweep down and across the outstretched arms while she recites the Apostolic Creed. This is said to allay the fear of the patient and thus lulls him to sleep — and heal him from "susto."

When the soul is said to be frightened or paralyzed, it is called "Espanto." The cure is the same as for "susto." Most curanderos are called "Don" or "Dona" before their first names. They generally do not charge, but expect a gift such as a chicken, tamales, fruit, etc.

Among the many superstitions are such as if you dream that a bird hits the windshield while driving, someone of the family will die, or when someone must climb through a window he has to come back the same way or Grandma will die. Also it is believed if someone dies leaving a debt, his soul will have no rest until the next of kin pays it.

It was the Thursday before Good Friday and Henry Esau heard his pupils saying, "Tonight and tomorrow we can't take any bath." "Why not?" he asked. "Because," one answered. "Because what?" he asked. Finally one girl blurted it out, "If I take a bath tonight or tomorrow, I will turn into half fish and half girl." "Who told you that?"

he asked, surprised. "Grandma," she answered. "Do you believe it?" "Yes," was her prompt reply. Later another Christian teacher told the following story. The children of a primary grade in another school also were concerned about not taking a bath on Thursday and Friday before Easter. She told them she would prove to them it is only a story. After Easter vacation she walked into her classroom saying, "See, children, nothing happened to me and I took a bath." "Miss, you did not." "Of course, I did," she responded. Then in a chorus they shouted, "Prove it, Miss."

There are very many other superstitions people fear and believe. It is as Harry Neufeld wrote about the unsaved, saying, "They are bound by superstitions and by peculiar beliefs that chain them to a constant fear of something that will bring harm to them. This fear does not allow them to step out boldly into the freedom of the Gospel of Christ." But thanks be to God who can and does give victory to all who believe in Jesus Christ as their Savior.

Another thing missionaries had to learn is that words have different meanings to Mexican Americans than they do to them. For example, the word "Jew" is the name given to persons who have not been baptized. A young man who had recently trusted Christ, read a few verses of the Bible in Sunday School class and said, "It makes no sense." Mrs. Esau asked, "Is it the word 'Jew'?" "Yes," he responded. She explained in the Bible the word "Jew" refers to the children of Abraham, Isaac and Jacob, also called Israel. "Well, then it does make sense," he answered. The word "grace" also presents a problem because to many it does not mean the unmerited favor of God, but the merits of Mary.

Workers have to learn not to offend a Mexican by asking, "Are you a Christian?" He will reply, "Of course I am; I was baptized. Am I an animal?" But if the missionary asks, "Are you a believer?", the response may be "A believer in what?" It thus opens the way to witness.

To Anglos it is a disrespect to God to call a boy by the name of "Jesus" or "Savior," but to Mexicans it is an honor to the saints to name their children after them. Just as the languages differ so are the minds and the ways of thinking of Anglos and Mexicans distinctly different. The sooner both races learn and accept this fact and try to understand each other, the better they will get along with each other.

Another thing the missionaries learned was to eat and like Mexican foods. They also learned to make tortillas and like them with pinto beans. One native worker told Anna Esau, "We Mexican people have made one contribution to America, that is our white wheat tortilla." The Mexican white corn tortilla is still used in making many other delicious foods. These corn tortillas require a long process to make. Corn is cleaned, soaked and boiled with slack lime until soft, and then washed and ground to make a masa (dough) from which tortillas are made as well as tamales. Foods containing onion or garlic, peppers and camino spice are considered authentic Mexican foods.

Many of the modern Mexican American cooks now buy the tortilla or the masa from bakeries or factories, instead of making it from scratch as did their grandmothers.

CHAPTER 2

EARLY EVENTS THAT LED TO THE OPENING OF THE FIELD IN SOUTH TEXAS

A. EARLY WORK OF MENNONITE BRETHREN THAT LED TO A MISSION AMONG MEXICAN PEOPLE

A number of Mennonite Brethren families mostly from Corn, Oklahoma, had moved to Premont, Texas, a hundred miles north of the Rio Grande River. Elder H.H. Flaming and others served in the church that was organized. Among them was Peter E. Penner, a well-known Bible expositor, who became especially burdened for the Mexican people. P.E. Penner later returned to the Valley and preached and handed out tracts. He used a young native, Ricardo Pena, to interpret for him. Assisted by Rev. and Mrs. Henry Andres, Penner's sister, they began colportage work. They visited the cities and villages in the Rio Grande Valley and also conducted Sunday schools with Spanish-speaking people in and around Premont. Rev. Penner conducted series of Bible studies in many of the Mennonite Brethren Southern District churches. He always presented the great need to evangelize the neglected people along the Rio Grande.

To further his work, Rev. P.E. Penner found men who shared his concern. Therefore, on December 16, 1927, at Rock Island, Colorado County, Texas, they incorporated the "John 3:16 Frontier Mission" for the purpose of getting Bibles and Christian literature into the hands of Spanish-speaking people. Rev. Penner owned a 50-acre tract of land near Encino, Texas, which he gave to the mission. Later the land was sold, but the mineral rights were kept. Money from the oil lease has provided funds to buy Bibles and other literature. All through the years of El Faro School as well as in the churches, Bibles were provided through this organization. Henry F. Reist, Premont, served until 1960 when he turned the distribution work over to Henry T. Esau, who by that time had moved to the Valley. Henry Esau served until his death. Later the work was passed on to his son, Kenneth L. Esau, and his wife Anna. Part of the price of the land is still in savings. From the interest and royalty from an oil lease plus donations, the work still keeps on going. Bibles are given free when the recipient is unable to pay anything, otherwise a donation is expected to keep a fund on hand.

Peter Penner kept on working as long as he could to stir up interest for a mission among Mexican Americans. The Board of Foreign Missions had begun a work among Mexicans at Lawton, Oklahoma, as a branch of Post Oak (the mission to the Comanche Indians), the first field to be opened by the American Mennonite Brethren in 1894.

13

While God was preparing a conference to send forth workers, He had been leading Harry Neufeld from Reedley, California, to be the very one to become the first missionary in South Texas. He had been saved at the age of sixteen and at once felt the urge to serve the Lord. He attended Bible school in Los Angeles and became useful in the Watchman's Club, a young men's organization. Then in 1924 his call to work among Mexican people came as a dream which he could not forget. He dreamt he was preaching to a large audience of Roman Catholics which resulted in him being imprisoned, but many souls were saved. He really did not believe in dreams and could not understand it, but could not get rid of it either. For years it caused him concern and gave him a special love for Mexican people around him. He began to study books which he obtained from a priest which increased his longing to present the true gospel to them.

Harry was led to Tabor College where he continued his education and met Sarah Kornelsen, whom he married in 1932. Years went by and they worked where the Lord led, but the vision for preaching to the Spanish-speaking did not open up until 1936. H.W. Lohrenz, secretary of the Foreign Mission Board, approached Harry Neufeld if he and his wife would be willing to enter a work among Mexican people. "Yes" was his answer.

Sarah Neufeld says, "At the Conference in Fairview, Oklahoma that fall, the proposition to open work in South Texas was presented and accepted with enthusiasm. And before we hardly knew what was happening, we were designated to go find a field along the Mexican border in Texas and start working. Harry was encouraged."

That school year, 1936-37, Harry finished his work toward his Th.B. at Tabor College. Their faith was tested when Sarah had to have surgery and had a long, slow convalescence. Nevertheless, by the summer of 1937 they were ready to go locate a field.

While Harry Neufeld was a student at Tabor College, he was invited to conduct a series of revival meetings at Premont. While there the challenge to evangelize the Mexican American people was renewed. He continued his studies while he and the people at Premont prayed for workers.

There were two sin-hardened men in Los Ebanos, Texas, now willing and waiting for someone to show the way. Also three Methodists and one Baptist, then living in that village, were praying, planning, and wishing that God might send someone there to begin a work of the Lord. Also in Falfurrias a dear sister, Mrs. Henry Andres, sister of Peter Penner, prayed and agonized for missionaries to go to this place.

God heard those sighs and prayers and His Holy Spirit worked in hearts of brethren who had come to attend the 1936 Southern District Conference of Mennonite Brethren of North America. The late Brother H.W. Lohrenz, secretary of the Foreign Mission Board, presented the need of mission work among Mexicans. The Lord warmed hearts and to the surprise of Brother Lohrenz the Southern District took it upon itself to open a mission to the Mexican people. Harry Neufeld says, "Those two men at Los Ebanos were the nucleus of God's working at the very time the decision was made in Fairview, Oklahoma, to send missionaries to the Valley. It was as the Macedonian cry to Paul of old, 'Come over and help us.' And instantly the missionaries were sent 1,000 miles in answer to that call by the Lord." Harry and Sarah Neufeld were the first workers set aside to become missionaries for the Mennonite Brethren Church to work among Mexican Americans in Texas.

B. THE OPENING OF A FIELD FOR MENNONITE BRETHREN AMONG MEXICAN AMERICANS

During the summer of 1937 Harry and Sarah Neufeld went to South Texas to find a field to begin the greatest soul winning adventure the Southern District of Mennonite Brethren had ever undertaken. Many souls are now in glory and the living believers thank God He gave vision to men of the Southern District and courage to begin a work in which no one else up to that time had succeeded. Those then on the Mission Committee were A.P. Epp, J.W. Vogt, and P.C. Hiebert.

The Neufelds left Hillsboro, Kansas, in a 1931 Chevrolet coupe pulling a small trailer house. They came down U.S. Highway 281 and first stopped in Premont, Texas. There they conducted some meetings for Mexican Americans. Harry Neufeld read to them from a Spanish translation of one of D.L. Moody's books. At the end of three days Mexicans came and pressed the missionaries' hands, threw their arms about them in embrace, and pleaded for them to return for more gospel messages.

Next the Neufelds journeyed down to the Rio Grande Valley proper. They came to Edinburg, Texas, the gateway to the Valley and made inquiry at the parsonage of the First Baptist Church. Among other things they were told, "If you people have decided to go to the border towns and villages, let me tell you one thing. You will appear to those people as foreign devils."

Quoting Harry Neufeld, "Although the entire border was canvassed in order to find a field of missionary labors for the Mennonite Brethren Church of North America, the final establishment of this enterprise was in the villages just west of Mission, Texas." They are Abram, Penitas, La Joya, Havana, Los Ebanos, Cuevitas, La Grulla, Garciasville-Casita and smaller scattered settlements reaching to Rio Grande City. These villages up to that time had never been truly evangelized nor had the knowledge of salvation in Jesus Christ been presented to their people. The Neufelds returned to Kansas and reported to the Southern District Conference of 1937. They were asked to go to Texas and develop a field for Mennonite Brethren.

C. THE SPIRITUAL CONDITIONS OF THE PEOPLE OF THE VILLAGES BETWEEN MISSION AND RIO GRANDE CITY

The people living hidden in smaller and larger villages were seldom seen by tourists who traveled along U.S. Highway 83. They had no system of government except some chosen by the priests to look after the cemeteries. There was at least one cantina (saloon) or more in each village where drunken men shot or stabbed each other. Texas Rangers patrolled the border constantly; nevertheless, they did not interfere with their domestic lives.

These village people were also neglected by the very church that had baptized them. The churches in the villages also were in a sad condition. A priest would come one or more times a year to baptize the babies born since his last visit. He conducted doctrinal classes to prepare children to pray the rosary and take their first communion. He also listened to all who came to confess so they could receive the holy communion. After the children had learned to pray the rosary and went to confess the first time, there was a great festival in the church. Little girls all dressed as brides and boys all in white received their first communion. Then in each home there would be a feast of all the best the family could provide. This, for the most part, was all the people learned. If they went to confession once a year, they were in good standing with the church.

Each village had some women who would go conduct or say the rosary when someone died. In early years no priest came, so the villagers buried their dead on the "Campo Santo" (Holy Ground) with only the saying of the rosary.

The people were either negligent, did little praying at home or were very religious. There was an altar in each home. It might be only a corner shelf on which the saints were kept. Some had only a crucifix and a few saints while others had every saint they could buy on large altars or on the wall of a room. Fresh flowers with candles were set before the images and pictures of the saints, called "santitos", or little saints. That is where the people prayed and made their vows. They very seldom would break a vow. There are very many "virgins" who are as "Mary." She may be fair or brown, blue-eyed or dark-eyed. Anna Esau asked a girl in Premont, "How can Mary be fair and also brown?" "Well," she explained, shrugging her shoulders, "that is simple. She appears that way." "So she can change herself as she wishes?" was the next question. "Yes, she has that power and she can do anything." Another example of their spiritual blindness is shown in the following incident. One day two boys came to the Esaus' home at Premont. They talked about the "saints" and especially the "virgin." So Anna Esau asked them, "Do you really pray to the paper and the paint of the saint?" "No, we don't," they promptly responded. "What then do you pray to?" she inquired. "The real one." "Who is the real one?" she continued. "Well, it is her spirit," they answered. "But God says in His Word, He does not live in things made by the hands of men," she responded. They had never heard that so could not understand. In their minds, to pray before a saint was praying to God.

As soon as the Gospel of Jesus Christ was preached in a village, people began to work and restore their old churches or build new ones. The visits of the priests also became more frequent. People were put to the test to believe the Word of God or go on as they had for centuries. Giving the people the opportunity to receive or reject the Gospel of Jesus Christ is evangelizing. The M.B. Southern District through its missionaries has done a great work of evangelizing from 1937 to 1969. Only eternity will reveal how many have been saved from lives of fear and superstition to the glorious hope which is in Christ Jesus.

D. THE VILLAGE OF LOS EBANOS

The village of Los Ebanos was named after the Texas Ebony (not an ebony, for it belongs to the bean family). The ebony is the Valley's longest living and largest hardwood plant. Los Ebanos lies on the bank of the Rio Grande which makes a sudden turn into Mexico; thus the village has the river on three sides at the lower end. It never was planned, for its streets run every which way, because it grew just like its families. In 1937 most homes were small, although in line along a given street. For the greater part the houses were humble and unpainted, but their yards were neatly kept. There were some buildings built of brick which enterprising citizens made of the river clay. The villagers loved plants and beauty, so each one had what he could take care of. Water was the greatest problem. Four families had windmills that pumped water from wells. The rest had to buy their water if it did not rain to keep their barrels filled. Water was hauled for a few cents by a native boy on a barrel cart pulled by a donkey. The Neufelds had some water piped to their house from a neighbor's supply tank, but it was very slow running. So their drinking water was in a barrel on the porch. After three years the Neufelds purchased a butane tank and cook-stove. They also were the first to acquire a kerosene refrigerator and soon the storekeepers followed suit. After that folks could buy fresher produce. The people used kerosene or gasoline lamps in their homes and at night the streets were always dark.

Electricity came in 1946, but water and gas came later. With the coming of modern utilities, much changed in the village. Since then new and beautiful modern homes have been built.

The streets were dusty during dry seasons and muddy during wet ones so they were gravelled. The gravel had rather large rocks in it so the streets were bumpy. By 1937 there were very few cars to rumble over the stones. More owned trucks to haul migrants who left for the harvesting seasons in other places up north.

The people farmed the lowlands with primitive tools and worked for the Anglo ranchers as often as they could. For many life was a battle for existence, especially those families where the breadwinner spent much time in the cantinas (saloons). As in all races some were more thrifty than others. But in many homes the mothers and older children all went out to work in the fields to help support the ever growing families.

CHAPTER 3

LOS EBANOS, THE FIRST MENNONITE BRETHREN MISSION ALONG THE RIO GRANDE

A. THE LOS EBANOS STATION

The first services were conducted January 23, 1938 in an old windowless structure made of brick, which the church rented. A year later some openings were cut through the walls and windows were installed. Gasoline lamps were used until Sarah's brother, Jacob, sent a small generator, which they used for the house.

In 1942 the Conference allotted $450.00 for the construction of a new church in Los Ebanos. Church members from Premont came off and on to help and sometimes Harry worked alone. The floor was laid by Federico Peña. The church was dedicated on March 29, 1942. The cost of the building was $736.00. Premont church members came to help celebrate. A tower was added in 1951 to complete the church.

In 1944 Miguel Carrizales, a Methodist Christian who owned a lumber yard, donated a little more than half an acre of land for the parsonage in Los Ebanos. There had been an old brick factory on the land. The ruined factory had to be bulldozed before the building could begin. The Neufelds planned the house, but had construction help from a local carpenter, who served as contractor. The work was done by the Neufelds with help from Henry Thomas, the new missionary at Chihuahua, as well as others.

Construction did not proceed uninterrupted. Harry had trouble with his back and Sarah was ill for some time. The first well was unsatisfactory and another had to be dug. A windmill was built but, for lack of steady wind, it was inadequate. A pressure pump had to be installed. When it was finished, the Neufelds had a comfortable home and, with the addition of electricity and butane, living became quite modern. This house is still standing, located on the main road into Los Ebanos, about two blocks east of where the church was built.

Trees, shrubs and flowers decorated the old brick factory site, the parsonage served the workers at Los Ebanos and was home for the Alfredo Tagles long after the merger of the La Joya, Chihuahua and Los Ebanos churches.

While Harry was still at Los Ebanos, the church built another block structure to serve as a center for Sunday school and youth activities, as well as the women's work.

Later the church was dismantled after the congregation began to attend at La Joya. The block building and the lots were sold and the money used in building the new church in La Joya.

B. THE WORK OF THE LOS EBANOS CHURCH

The first church services were very simple, comprised of singing, memory work, testimonies and preaching. The Neufelds did everything until there were others to help. As people joined the church Ricardo Zapata, only 17, became Sunday school superintendent. Another early worker was Ricardo Peña, who became a missionary in 1947. Others who were among the first to join were Abelardo Mireles, the very first person baptized (on June 5, 1938), and Ricardo's parents, Frederico and Maria Luisa.

C. THE WORK AMONG THE YOUNG PEOPLE
AND CHILDREN AT LOS EBANOS

Harry and Sarah Neufeld paid special attention to the young people that had joined or were coming to the various activities. Something special was done with the youth and children every Christmas, Easter and Mother's Day. Programs were presented by Sunday school classes; many mothers attended, including those who otherwise did not come to the church. By May, 1955, there was a boys' club, the only one in the Valley then, named "Sky Pilots." Under the slogan: "It is better to build boys than to mend men," the club's aim was to counter delinquency and to implant in the boys the desire to become missionaries at home, school and the playground. The organization's headquarters was in San Jose, California.

Harry and Sarah also had a young people's choir and did plays such as "The Shoemaker" and the "Challenge of the Cross" in Spanish, as well as shorter ones, which the young people performed in other churches. Sometimes they sang and performed outside at Cuevitas, Abram and Garciasville. They once did the "Challenge of the Cross" in English in Premont.

Sarah had a Pioneer Girls' Club, where the girls sang, heard a Bible lesson, did crafts and earned badges. They learned how to work together and also how to live a life that counted for Christ.

There also was a club for younger girls called Busy Bees. They sang and listened to Bible stories. Other workers were Otila Villarreal from Los Ebanos and Alvina (Fast) Boese, a teacher at El Faro. Otila had Sunday night classes for the children for a while.

Daily Vacation Bible Schools were held at Los Ebanos and various other locations each year. The Bible was taught to many young people, many of whom were not permitted to attend regular church services.

D. THE WORK AMONG WOMEN AT LOS EBANOS

To strengthen the church, Harry and Sarah believed it was very important to help believing mothers to reach their children and husbands for the Lord. Sarah set aside Wednesdays for Bible classes, first in the homes of the women, later in her own house and then in the Sunday school building that was built near the church. She had a class in Cuevitas and, a few times, at Havana. She later went to Cuevitas and Sullivan to pick up the women and brought them to Los Ebanos, taught the class, then took them home. They studied the Bible, memorized verses and prayed. During the last years of the Neufeld's ministry, the women also made quilts, which were sold to support a Bible ministry in India. Except on special occasions, such as Christmas, they served no refreshments. At Christmas they made plates of food and took them to selected homes, presented a short Gospel message and sang. This was well received to be honored in such a loving way. After the Los Ebanos church acquired a van, Sarah Neufeld also took them to other places.

The work among the women became the best way to reach the homes. Ofelia Tagle was the last one at Los Ebanos to guide the women's group and inspire them with new ideas, before the church merged with La Joya and Chihuahua.

E. WORK AMONG THE SICK AT LOS EBANOS

Few people had cars during those early years of work in Los Ebanos, so the Neufelds were often called to take people to the doctor. Harry spent considerable time and effort the first year trying to find help for Federico Peña, who had a baffling illness. They were also frequently exposed to tuberculosis; a neighbor with TB often visited their house. Says Sarah: "How could I tell her not to come? And the Lord miraculously spared us."

A few times they stayed up all night with very ill persons and, on one occasion, dared to go to the home of a very antagonistic family whose daughter was believed to be dying. They prayed for the very ill girl; she recovered and the parents later brought her to the missionary's house to show that she was well. The Neufelds prayed with them again.

F. A TRANSPORTATION PROBLEM SOLVED
AT LOS EBANOS

Harry and Sarah were alone for five years but, with local help, they visited many villages and ranches. Harry conducted as many as seven services a week in various villages and ranches. People were saved here and there, but it was impossible to minister in so many places. The mission was about four years old when the Neufelds and the Mission Board decided to get a bus. Harry bought a 1936 Chevrolet panel truck, cut two windows on each side and made benches along the sides. It seated about twenty youngsters. On the side he painted "Los Ebanos Sunday School Bus;" a picture of an open Bible was painted just back of the driver's seat. The bus attracted the attention of the local paper, which printed an article and picture of the Neufelds and Gordon standing beside it. It was believed to be the only bus of its kind in the Valley at that time.

As the work grew the bus was cut in two and expanded about two feet. This gave room for a third bench in the middle. The top was painted silver to reflect the heat and it received the name "Canosa," or the "gray-headed lady." This was the first bus on the mission field in South Texas.

Another bus was soon needed to get all the people who wanted to come to the services. A third was donated by A.F. Penner of Hillsboro, Kansas. The "Canosa" served until it was replaced by a real bus in 1948. It was used at the new station at Premont, where it served until a larger bus was needed. It was then sent back to the Valley.

G. REVIVAL SERVICES AND EXTENSION WORK BY LOS EBANOS WORKERS

Harry Neufeld believed in revival services and held the first of many in May, 1938, his first year of work in Los Ebanos. Special services were conducted for two weeks by Salvador Rivera of the Lawton Mission; it was also at this time that Rivera and Neufeld translated the Mennonite Brethren Confession of Faith into Spanish.

Extension work occurred when Neufeld and Inocencio Garcia of the Chihuahua village preached at La Paloma near Brownsville. They also visited the Methodists in Rio Grande City and received permission to use their little chapel in Garciasville, where Ricardo Peña and others began Mennonite Brethren church work.

Church members also broadcast the gospel message in the villages of Cuevitas, Chihuahua, Abram, Garciasville and on ranches. They went as far as Fronton, west of Roma, and to a ranch north of Sullivan City. Other workers who followed continue to evangelize the people in and about the village of Los Ebanos.

H. THE STORE AT LOS EBANOS

The various Women's Mission Circles of the Southern District gathered and repaired used clothing and baby layettes, quilts and comforters. During the early years the gifts were all sent to Los Ebanos, where they were sold. It was a good way to reach people who would not come to church and some friendships were made through the store. Money earned through sales was invested in the mission. Although the store initially took much of Sarah's time, other workers later each spent time in the store.

I. OPPOSITION TO THE GOSPEL AT LOS EBANOS

When people have lived from generation to generation all belonging to the same church, there is religious peace. In Los Ebanos they also believed the Mexican saying, "Each head is its own world." They granted each citizen to live as he chose, worship one or many saints, or have none, go to church or not to go, live a life of vice or to be an honorable citizen, just as long as he or she did not join another church.

People were saved soon after the Neufelds came to Los Ebanos. On June 5, 1938, Abelardo Mireles, Sr. was the very first to be baptized. This caused a stir. People saw how he had changed, but they still felt it their duty to keep him from the Mennonite Brethren Church. He was sorely tested, but did not yield; soon more were baptized. Young Ricardo Peña was in the next group to be baptized, and his parents followed later.

But there was opposition; in his book, *Eight Years Among Latin-Americans,* Neufeld says, "Some who did not attend the evangelical services tried in every way possible to hinder others. Before church services they stationed themselves on strategic corners of the plaza and, as the children and adults came along on their way to the chapel, they pulled them back and told them not to go there. They slandered the missionary and his purpose. Others came to the services with their pockets loaded with firecrackers. They stuck them into cracks of the walls on the outside, lit them and ran. You can imagine the noise that followed. Others played baseball right in front of the little gathering place, trying to distract and lure children and young people from the services."

Most of the village men never went to church, although some girls and women did. Girls were organized into clubs which vied with one another to try and disturb the evangelical meetings. They formed religious processions, carrying pictures of the Virgin Mary and the crucifix and sometimes pictures of a patron saint. All carried candles, walking through the streets, chanting prayers and singing songs to the saints and the Virgin Mary. They stopped in front of the little chapel, made as much noise as they could and shouted pronouncements of a ban on all who left the mother church.

The leaders, fearing that more people would attend evangelical services, became active and inspired the people to rebuild their old churches. In villages where there had never been a church, new ones were built. Special meetings were held to revive their faith and warn the people. They were told to drive the missionary and his family out because they were devils and taught the doctrine of the devil. But many people had learned to know the Neufelds as true friends in times of trouble and disregarded the warnings.

J. MISSIONARIES, PASTORS AND OTHER WORKERS AT LOS EBANOS

Harry and Sarah Neufeld moved to Los Ebanos in January, 1938. For five years they served alone, ministering in many areas; when others came, they confined the work to Los Ebanos. In 1951-52, while they enjoyed a furlough, Ricardo and Grace Hiebert Zapata came to serve at Los Ebanos in their absence. After the year away they served five more years. In the summer, 1957, all the churches were invited to a festival. It was a day of rejoicing yet sorrow when the Neufelds left to pastor the Sunset Garden Mission Church in Fresno, CA. In

August, 1973, they returned for a visit, together with Gordon and his family. They were warmly received. It was a special time for Harry, since he knew he had cancer; he was able to minister in the churches one more time. He was called home November 21, 1973, after a rich life of service for the Lord.

Alfredo Tagle was the first Mexican American pastor at Los Ebanos. As a young man he left the Lull church near Edinburg and went to Los Ebanos on August 16, 1957. After Eugene and Lillian Janzen came in March, 1958, the Mission Board asked Alfredo to stay to help them learn Spanish and help them with the work. He left in May, 1958.

Eugene and Lillian Janzen of Fairview, Oklahoma, replaced the Neufelds. They did good work during their two years of ministry. They returned to Oklahoma in June, 1960.

Noe Ortiz, a Mexican educated in the United States, came to Los Ebanos in September, 1960, from the Rio Grande Bible Institute. During his stay he taught the members that they all had to do their part since Los Ebanos no longer was a mission. Ortiz left in August, 1961, to pastor a Baptist Church.

When school started in fall, 1961, Tim and Myrna Nickel Kliewer came to live in the parsonage at Los Ebanos. He preached in English with parts interpreted for the sake of those who understood only Spanish. When they moved to Mission during the second semester, Paul and Donna-Beth Wiebe served as pastor couple. They also did not know Spanish. The next year Tim Kliewer served the church and taught in El Faro. At the end of summer, 1963, they moved to California where Myrna entered nurses' training and Tim acquired his Masters degree from the Mennonite Brethren Biblical Seminary in Fresno.

José and Graciela Lara were from Tamasunchale, Mexico, but knew English. In 1963 they were asked to take over the Los Ebanos church. He also taught in El Faro for two years. He was the third Mexican-American to carry on the work at Los Ebanos. They left in 1965.

Alfredo and Ofelia Tagle moved from La Grulla, where they had worked for a number of years, to Los Ebanos on August 1, 1965. They served until 1968, when the church merged with La Joya and Chihuahua. Alfredo was not the pastor when the Los Ebanos church decided to go to La Joya, but he was asked to serve by the united La Joya church group. Years later, in 1984, German Contreras lived in the parsonage in Los Ebanos and began services for people who did not attend at La Joya or any other church.

K. TWO CONVERSION STORIES

A closed jail door became an open door to the gospel for Abelardo Mireles. Although he had been raised by religious parents, he quickly forgot their instruction. He ran with the wrong crowd, almost killed a man in a gun battle and, together with Federico Peña, was a smuggler and bootlegger. In 1935 he opened a saloon in Los Ebanos; in 1937 he was sentenced to 50 days in jail for smuggling and selling illegal liquor.

While in jail he was visited by some Christians and, for the first time, Abelardo heard the gospel. He left jail with a desire to know more about Jesus. When Harry and Sarah Neufeld visited the Mireles home for the first time that year, they found an open door. During the second visit Abelardo accepted Christ as his saviour. He was baptized on June 5, 1938, together with his son, Eliseo.

Harry remembers that a "marvelous change" occurred to Abelardo. Where he had once been hard and rough, he was, after his conversion, soft, tender-hearted and kind. He was ostracized by his family for his new faith, despite the positive changes; in spite of the opposition he lovingly won his wife and most of his children to Christ, together with other relatives.

Unlike Abelardo Mireles, Federico Peña's parents were not very religious. Federico Peña, who was born in San Miguel, was baptized as an infant, but religion was not prominent in his life. At the age of eight, Federico began drinking and, like a monster, the vice coiled itself around him.

When he was fourteen, his father passed away and, since he was the oldest, he had to quit school to provide for his mother and five siblings. He worked as a carpenter.

Alcohol, however, soon dominated his whole life and by twenty he was an habitual drunkard. At times he would not be sober once during a week. He drank almost every day in the year. On the night of his marriage to Maria Luisa Flores, he was so drunk he hardly knew his name.

His drinking was hard on his family. Many a night his wife sent the four boys out of the house to keep them from harm. Despite his drunkenness, he became concerned about his four boys — they were growing up and he really did not want his way of life passed on to them. He also began to regret how terribly he was living. So, he reasoned, "Surely God is a good God or else he could not protect me after I have sinned so against Him."

In 1932 the Peña family moved to Los Ebanos, Texas and met Mrs. Sarah Carrizales, a believer then living in Los Ebanos. She often spoke to Federico and asked him to buy a Bible and read it, but he refused. Then, one day, she stuck a Bible into his hand and told him to read it, saying that if he did not like it, he could return it without paying. He never returned it — he read it and began to want more and more of it each day. In 1937 he heard Harry Neufeld preach in Los Ebanos at the village school house. Unknown to the Neufelds, Federico and his wife accepted Christ, because they wanted to be examples to their boys.

When Harry and Sarah Neufeld returned to begin the mission work at Los Ebanos, Federico and his family were among the first supporters. Everyone in the village noticed the change in his life and was surprised. By the time the Neufelds came, Federico had read much of the Bible, which he took with him wherever he went. All who came in contact with him had to listen to his message from his precious book. He proved he had been born again.

Federico's new faith was tested with a strange disease. Like Job of old, even his friends turned against him, saying, "This is what you get for becoming a Protestant." They scoffed at him, but he stood firm and replied, "I will never leave my God no matter if I have to suffer much more than this."

The disease was diagnosed as leprosy. Ricardo says the prayers of the believers were answered and the Lord healed him. For years he and his wife ran a grocery story in Los Ebanos, remaining faithful witnesses to the end.

CHAPTER 4

THE MENNONITE BRETHREN
MISSION AT CHIHUAHUA

A. EARLY EVENTS THAT LED TO THE OPENING
OF A STATION AT CHIHUAHUA

Chihuahua is a word that no one seems to know the meaning of, although many use it as an expression of surprise or annoyance. In the village of Abram, two miles from Chihuahua, lived a family whose daughter, Marta, was ill. She was advised to seek help from curanderos — healers who claim to cure people by magic powers. When these did not help, she was told to seek help from the saints, a special saint was given to her, and candles were kept burning night and day about her bed. It was to no avail; she just became worse. One day while kneeling before her crucifix and patron saint, a conviction came over her: "These things are dead and they cannot help me," she thought. She took them off the altar and, casting them into another room, said, "I'm going to see a doctor." The doctor advised an immediate operation.

When she entered the hospital, she was asked to which religion she belonged. "I don't know," she responded. "I was a Catholic, but now I guess I am nothing." The nurse, not knowing what to do, put her down as a Catholic. As a result a priest called upon her and asked if she had a confession to make.

She replied, "I am going to make my confession in five days after my operation, if I am well enough. Come in at that time."

The operation was a success and on the fifth day the priest came, asking for her confession.

"My confession is simply this," she told him. "I have sought help in the principles and doctrines I have known all my life and have found none. Now I am going to get a Bible and read it, find God's plan for my soul and get rid of my burdens. This is my last confession."

The priest was surprised, but told her, "If you feel that way about it, go ahead and get a Bible. But don't tell anyone why you did it."

During her stay in the hospital she met Christian nurses who told her more about the new way of life. She promised herself that she would join the first evangelical church that would help her find the true way to Christ. Abelardo Mireles Sr. heard about her quest and told Harry Neufeld; together they went to Abram and conducted their first evangelical service at the home of Inocencio Garcia's grandfather, on September 29, 1938. Marta, who was there, was saved. Neufeld remembers that "It was a great joy to preach to this soul that evening in fellowship with some other relatives." After the service she spoke with a beaming face. "Friends," she said, "this is what my heart has been longing for all these years. Now I have found that for which I have been seeking." Later, in 1940, she was the first one to be baptized and become a member of the Chihuahua Church. She witnessed for her Lord and won others to Him.

When José Garcia heard about Marta's conversion, he was happy, and invited the Neufelds and Mireles to come to Chihuahua. José and his wife had come to Chihuahua in 1938, when she had had a dream. "Take your family and move west to a place where you find an old school house." She thought that the dream meant that they would find work and a better place to live and, possibly, a chance to testify for the Lord. The family decided to move to a ranch about four miles west of Mission, Texas. But she still felt an urge within herself to move on. As a result, they moved about one mile further west, to a place surrounded by brush and wild life. They lived alone in a former school house — it was dilapidated and dust and rain came in at will. There were no close neighbors but, nevertheless, they felt that they had followed the Lord's leading.

They sent a message to the Neufelds and Mireles: "Come over to us also." During that time P.E. Penner came to the Valley and Harry Neufeld showed him about. A stop at the Garcia home for prayer and a message was the first meeting at Chihuahua. It ultimately led to large open air meetings and then a church.

B. THE CHIHUAHUA STATION

During November, 1940, Harry Neufeld bought an old house in Abram for $20.00. It was taken apart and moved to Chihuahua and set up again on a lot near the road. This was used until it became too small and a larger church was built for $130.00 in 1941. Harry Neufeld and Eliseo Mireles painted the new church; over the door they placed a sign which said, "The Church of the Lord of the Mennonite Brethren." A mesquite tree stood just in front and many other large mesquites shaded the yard. The church was dedicated on April 27, 1941.

The members were happy to have their own church. Henry and Ruth Thomas arrived on December 4, 1942, as their missionaries. The church grew so rapidly that the building had to be enlarged in 1944. A few years later more room was needed; the old church was moved back under the big trees and a larger new one was built.

On March 18, 1946, A.W. Epp, A.B. Kliewer and Walter Bartel arrived to begin work at the church. The Ruben Wedels supplied the meals and hauled the water, while some native girls helped with the dishes. After Sunday school services, Rev. A.W. Epp preached, with Henry Thomas translating for him. More workers — Albert Epp, Edwin Kliewer, Ben Warkentine, Harrison Martens, and Clifford Just — came from Fairview, Oklahoma, a week later; they were joined by some of the Mexican American members. On April 28, 1946, the church was dedicated, although the inside was not all completed. The next summer, the Henry T. Esaus, from Long Island, Kansas, helped paint and varnish the woodwork.

Henry and Ruth Thomas tried to buy land in or near Chihuahua, but were unable to. Early in 1943, A.W. Epp and his brother-in-law, Henry Fast, bought a tract of land in Abram and donated two acres to the Southern District Conference. The Conference later bought a house on a citrus ranch northeast of Mission owned by D.T. Ediger of Buhler, Kansas. This house was moved to Abram and the Thomas' lived in it for a few years before it was enlarged and modernized. Palms, shrubs and grass beautified the place. It remained the parsonage as long as the Chihuahua church was in existence.

C. THE WORK OF THE CHIHUAHUA CHURCH AMONG CHILDREN AND YOUTH

The Sunday school was the first to be organized. For some years Henry Thomas did the work, but Inocencio Garcia was the first Sunday school superintendent and later became assistant pastor. The Thomas' both taught Sunday school classes. Others were drawn in to help teach classes for all ages.

Susie Martin, a teacher of El Faro, taught the only English Sunday school class in Chihuahua for eight years. She hitch-hiked to get from the school to the church until her family provided her with a car. She helped with various activities in the church. In 1955 the Thomas' and their deacon, Ernesto Andrade, and his wife, had Bible schools at three places with 250 children enrolled. Many of these were not permitted by their parents to attend Sunday school.

The church also operated Bible schools in summer for children whose parents had not gone away to find work during various harvests. Some years they divided the school and went to the ranches to teach children who lived there. Those were great times, singing, listening to Bible stories and doing some sort of handwork. For one school year Dolores Balzer played the piano for song services. Mexican Americans love to sing loudly and joyously.

Henry Thomas led the singing for the services and directed the youth choir. The children and young people always put on a good Christmas program. They had special events for Easter and Mother's Day, which always were well attended.

Ruth Thomas also had some club work with the girls. The girls came to sing, listen to a Bible story and do crafts. She also gave a Bible lesson or a story on Sunday evenings.

D. THE WORK AMONG WOMEN AT CHIHUAHUA

Ruth Thomas was especially interested in teaching the mothers, in order to win the families. She had home Bible classes in the villages and ranches. For a while, when she had help in the house, she taught six Bible classes per week. Many women, who would not come to church, came to the classes. One time, during prayer, one woman came and knelt down near Ruth and said, "I want to be saved." Because a number of mothers were saved, they won their husbands to the Lord. Henry Thomas says: "The Bible classes were a direct result of the growth of our church." Just before Christmas, Ruth had a party in her house for all members of her Bible classes. They were sure to come then, bringing many children. They did not mind missing school on that day.

Anna Esau was privileged to go along with Ruth one day and was impressed by the spirit of love and unity in the class.

E. WORK AMONG THE SICK AT CHIHUAHUA

Ruth Thomas was concerned about the health needs of her friends. She took many to doctors and to clinics. She also gave prescription injections to many who needed them.

Lupita Rodriquez had tuberculosis. She left the hospital and asked Ruth to give her the streptomycin shots. Ruth, concerned about her spiritual well-being, presented Christ to her. Lupita accepted the Lord and left a good testimony before she went home to be with Him in glory.

Consuelo Villarreal, a member of the church, was pregnant and Ruth took her to the clinic in Mission. She developed urenic poisoning, however, by the time the baby was delivered. It left her in a coma. Ruth took the baby, David, to Antonio and Matilda Garcia in Chihuahua, who were glad to take care of him. Since Consuelo did not get well, the doctor ordered her to be flown to Galveston's John Sealy Hospital for treatment. A small plane was hired and Ruth flew along to stand by while Consuelo was there. The Lord heard the prayers and blessed the treatment and Consuelo recovered.

Ruth Thomas also took care of a man who had jaundice and, because of this, became infected. She was ill and in need of rest so they were given a furlough in 1956. Ricardo and Carmen Peña moved to Abram and took charge of the church while they were gone.

F. THE WORK OF TRANSPORTATION

Since the Chihuahua congregation was widespread, the missionaries spent much time getting the people and then taking them home again after church services, club meetings and Bible classes. La Homa Ranch, for instance, was 10 miles from the church. Sometimes the bus went even further.

G. THE MISSIONARIES AND WORKERS OF CHIHUAHUA CHURCH

The Harry Neufelds were the first to go and conduct services at Chihuahua. They continued until Henry and Ruth Dick Thomas came to take over the work in 1942.

Henry Thomas came from Corn, Oklahoma. Ruth Dick was born in Saskatchewan, Canada, but grew up in Luster, Montana. Henry and Ruth met at Tabor College and were married August 7, 1938. Henry taught in western Kansas four years. They were accepted as missionaries by the 1942 Southern District Mennonite Brethren Conference. They arrived on the field in December, 1942, and were ordained for missionary service in the fall of 1943 at Corn, Oklahoma. Henry and Ruth served the Chihuahua church for seventeen years. They had three sons, Marlin, Dannie, and Arthur.

For one year, 1956-57, The Thomases were given a furlough, and Ricardo and Carmen Villareal Peña left La Joya and lived in Abram to serve the Chihuahua church.

The Thomases left Chihuahua in January, 1960, living in Corn, Oklahoma, until they moved to California. Ruth went home to be with the Lord on June 19, 1981. Henry later married Susie Martin.

After the Thomases left Chihuahua, the Mennonite Brethren Foreign Mission Board sent Daniel and Elsie Fidler Wirsche to help the Chihuahua church. The Wirsches, members of the Hepburn, Saskatchewan Mennonite Brethren Church, had four sons, Stanley, Wesley, Peter, and Donald. They later joined the Butler Avenue Church in Fresno, California. They were the first Mennonite Brethren missionaries to be sent to open a field in Colombia. They had also served at Nuevo Ideal in Mexico, so they came well qualified to help the Valley Mennonite Brethren Mission churches begin to function as a Conference.

The Wirsches came in January, 1960 and lived in McAllen, Texas, until July when they moved into the parsonage at Abram. They remodeled the house and carried on the various activities which the Thomas' had started. They also both taught in El Faro School, where Daniel also served as superintendent for most of their stay at Chihuahua. They left in March, 1968 and were sent to Montevideo, Uruguay to work and teach in the mission there. The Wirsches have returned several times for furloughs to spend a little time in their home at Citrus Mobile Home Park, Edinburg, Texas. After many years in Uruguay, they returned during the last days of November, 1983 to live in their own home and serve as the Lord would direct. They again left in February, 1984 to teach in the Bible School in Montevideo.

After Daniel and Elsie Wirsche left for Uruguay, the Chihuahua church was without a pastor. But God provided two members of the church, Antonio Garcia, a deacon, and Wesley Wirsche, Daniel and Elsie's son, to take over. They kept the church going until it merged with the La Joya and Los Ebanos churches. During that time, all helped to keep the various functions of the church going, with several members preparing messages and delivering them Sunday morning or evening.

When the merger came, the members went to La Joya. Their old white building in Chihuahua was taken down to help build a big new church in La Joya.

CHAPTER 5

THE MENNONITE BRETHREN CHURCH AT LA GRULLA

A. THE VILLAGE OF LA GRULLA

La Grulla (pronounced La "Gruya", meaning "the crane") is located twenty-one miles west of the old Chihuahua village, a few miles south of the Highway 83. In the area from Mission to Rio Grande City, La Grulla is the largest single village, as it was in 1945 when it had a population of 1,500. There was no evangelical church in it at that time; the Methodists had begun a church earlier but had discontinued the work, leaving a little deserted chapel and a few believers in the village.

Harry Neufeld considered it the hardest village in which to begin a new church. There was no chapel or congregation to welcome the coming of Ruben and Eva Wedel.

La Grulla had an old small church, to which priests came to minister to the people, but most never went to church except for special occasions. They worshipped at home.

In 1945 the condition of the village was as in others — homes were small and poorly constructed and the streets were in a poor condition.

B. EARLY BEGINNINGS OF THE WORK AT LA GRULLA

The first witnessing was done by going into homes and getting acquainted with the people or by befriending them on the streets. The first Sunday school classes were held in the home of Anita and Santos Guerra, two single Methodist ladies.

Miss Ruth Loewen from Hillsboro, Kansas, came to help in the first Bible school. It was hard to get going; it was a new idea and some parents objected and did not allow their children to attend. But a few children were able to come and, in time, there were 28 enrolled. At the end of the Bible school it was decided to have a picnic at Penitas Lake. But this also was too new an idea, and the children were not permitted to go with the exception of one little girl.

After Bible school, the children were invited to come to Sunday school for the first time. Twelve children came, all eager to sing and memorize a Bible verse and listen to a Bible story. This class was held outside under a tree. From this small beginning, the Sunday school grew until one of the group, Eleazar Lozano, became superintendent.

Then came an invitation to help at a funeral. A man, whose

mother had died, asked Ruben to assist at the cemetery. Upon inquiring, he learned that this woman had been a believer. The family lived in Edinburg, but all her relatives were in La Grulla, so she was buried there.

A large crowd had gathered to see what would happen at an evangelical funeral. The women of the family were present at the grave instead of staying home and wailing, as was the custom. This family had hope and openly proclaimed it. Ruben gave a short message and then a Baptist minister spoke words of comfort to the family and gave a salvation message. Many heard the gospel for the first time in La Grulla.

The first Christmas program was held in the new garage, with about one hundred in attendance. Some even stood outside to listen to the children sing and recite verses. Some of these continued to come to Sunday school, so the work grew.

At first Ruben did not know enough Spanish to teach a Sunday school class without someone interpreting. Yolanda Villarreal, shortly after becoming a Christian, studied the Sunday school lesson in Spanish and soon taught the adult class.

C. THE LA GRULLA M.B. STATION

After a farewell service at Bessie, Oklahoma, Ruben and Eva Wiens Wedel arrived on the field on September 14, 1945. On the next day after they reached Los Ebanos, there was a welcoming service for them.

For the first two months the Wedels lived in their trailer house at the missionary homes of Harry Neufeld and Henry Thomas.

In November the Wedels moved the trailer house on Mr. Martin Cavazos' place west of Rio Grande City. They parked there until after Christmas. During that time, they went to the home of Mrs. Elida Falcón to study Spanish conversation. Ruben and Eva had taken Spanish grammar while at Moody Bible Institute.

During the time the new church was built at Chihuahua, the Wedels parked their trailer in Chihuahua near the Sunday school house. In the house there was space to put up a table, some benches, a china cupboard, and a stove, making it a mess hall for those who came to build. The Wedels prepared the meals, purchased groceries, and hauled water to drink.

One Sunday afternoon, the workers and the Wedels drove to La Grulla to see the village and contact a few friends they had made through Mrs. Falcón.

While the workers were still there at Chihuahua, they and the missionaries met at the home of the Henry Thomas' and held a special prayer meeting for the new work to be started March 31, 1946. A.W. Epp gave a fitting message. Later, Bible verses were given to the Wedels to encourage them to enter the work, no matter what problems they might face.

As soon as possible the Wedels looked for land and found a suitable place on the main road leading into the village. The family was willing to sell one-and-a-half acres to the Conference in June, 1946. They parked their trailer just across the street while they worked on the place.

The first thing they did was to drill a well. They found good water and then they moved their trailer on to the land. The little two-room house at Chihuahua was taken to La Grulla. J.P. Kliewer and Dave Fast from Premont built a kitchen, loaded it on a truck, and moved it to La Grulla on June 6, 1946. This was the first missionary home in La Grulla. The next summer, the Wedels built a garage in which to conduct their services.

In 1951 the little house was moved once more to the south side near the garage and was included in the enlarged modern home.

In March, 1949 a 28 foot by 52 foot church was begun to the north of the house. Many came to help build from Cordel, Fairview, and Corn, Oklahoma. All had to be housed and fed while they worked. Lack of funds permitted them to finish only the framework that spring. This church had a seating capacity of 275, the largest one on the field up to that time. Just before Christmas, the building was completed on the inside. The church was dedicated January 22, 1950, and the Sunday school addition was dedicated May 30, 1954. Ruben Wedel later built a bus garage, which served various purposes. This building was changed into a craft house and Sunday school building during the time Frank Munoz was serving at La Grulla. All these buildings were used for years until they were replaced by new ones by the Mennonite Brethren Church of La Grulla.

May 9, 1971, was a great day when the La Grulla Church celebrated its twenty-fifth anniversary. The sanctuary had been paneled to beautify it. Ruben Wedel helped when he had time. It was a day of rejoicing for the church and Ruben and Eva Wedel.

During the time Paul Castillo served at La Grulla, the congregation dismantled the church building which had been built in 1949. The termites had been busy so the congregation decided to build a modern block church with a roomy Sunday school wing. Alvin Neufeld had drawn the plans and construction began in summer, 1978. Moises Gutierrez, Paul Castillo, the pastor, and Rolando Mireles were on the building committee. Some winter Texans such as Lewis Toews, Wallace Loewen and others assisted in the project. The church was completed and dedicated in March of 1979.

Three funerals had been held in the incompleted church while Paul Castillo was pastor. The church also took down the parsonage and built a new one. The La Grulla Jr. High School Vocational Class directed by José Angel Villarreal worked on the project. It was begun in 1982 and finished by June 1, 1983, just in time for the new pastor, Jose J. Delgados, to move in.

D. WORK AMONG THE CHILDREN

There were summer Bible schools each year. For the second school in 1947, Ruth Loewen and Viola Warkentin came to teach under the trees and in the garage. Neighbor children soon came and others were brought by car. The children continued to come to Sunday school and, as they in turn introduced the Wedels to other children and relatives, the work grew.

After Yolanda Villarreal was saved, she and Lupita Ortiz took training from Child Evangelism. Yolanda and Lupita had a burden for the many children in La Grulla and began classes to reach them in 1952. The Lord opened doors so that mothers who never came to Sunday school eagerly waited for the classes in their homes. Yolanda had classes on Monday, Tuesday and Wednesday after school hours in three different homes. Among these women was an illiterate mother of twenty children. She listened and one day she asked, "How can I receive what you have?" She was saved and then asked, "What can I do for the Lord?" She invited and testified to others in her simple way. In 1955 Yolanda joined the Wedels in Mexico to train workers. She also helped in Vacation Bible school and showed the teachers how to use visual aids to better explain the Bible stories. El Faro teachers later helped teach Vacation Bible schools in La Grulla.

E. EVANGELISM AT LA GRULLA CHURCH

The outstanding thing about work in La Grulla is that the first converts were not only girls and women — a number of boys were won to the Lord, together with a few men. More men were saved later. They braved taunts from the unsaved of the village for having left their native faith. In March, 1947, Walter Gomez conducted a week of revival services. During that time Yolanda and Carmen Villarreal were converted. Yolanda was so devoted to her Lord that she spent hours on her knees praying at her altar until she developed calluses.

Yolanda loved art and went to the Wedel's house to get some instruction. While she was working, she heard Ruben Wedel deal with a person and she listened. It was all very new, but it awakened a desire in her to hear more. When she heard of revival meetings, she decided to go. The sisters both went to the revival meetings to hear Walter Gomez preach in the garage. Carmen says, "I went only to have a good time. I cracked jokes and had all around me laughing. Then, when Yolanda went forward, I sneaked up from behind just to hear what they were telling those folks. I listened and then — a blank. I don't know what happened, but I suddenly noticed I was kneeling with others who were being dealt with."

The first twelve to be baptized were Yolanda and Carmen Villarreal, Cataline Ortiz, Anita Ortiz, Josefa Ortiz Garcia, Eva Ortiz, Hector and Eleazar Lozano, Ramon Zarate, Israel and Luis Garcia, and Ubaldo Ortiz. P.C. Hiebert from Hillsboro, Kansas, spoke at this baptism, held in the Lake of Penitas. That was a time of rejoicing and a church was founded which has survived and grown to the present day. The Ruben Wedels also went to witness at a ranch six miles north of the church. There was an open door and persons were saved. Some became workers of the church and still live there.

F. WORK AMONG YOUNG PEOPLE

The work among the young people was called Youth for Christ. In La Grulla about twenty met on Friday nights for singing, games and Bible study. Once a month the group and the sponsors gathered at El Faro School. They had various Bible contests besides recreation. Those were great days for the youth of the churches and lasting results remained. One native pastor's wife told Anna Esau, "I never knew Christians could have such a good clean time." John Savoia had a vision for the young people and did a great deal to foster spiritual growth in them. Savoia took the youth out Christmas caroling with ringing bells. The whole church was taken out to spend a day in the park.

G. WORK AMONG THE WOMEN

As soon as mothers were saved, they began to meet to pray, have devotions, and sew and make quilts. Many of these items were sold to raise some money to make improvements in the church or parsonage. This has continued through the years. A good sized group from the ranch six miles north have greatly strengthened the women's and the church work. Ofelia Tagle helped the women to organize and since then they have managed their own activities. While the Wedels served La Grulla, there were 12 to 15 women active in this work. This organization is still going forward and greatly helps the church. Ofelia Tagle was a great help to bring many new ideas to the group. She taught Bible classes and her enthusiasm and various gifts greatly encouraged the work among the women.

H. WORK OF HELPING THE NEEDY

During those early years there were many very poor people, and one way to help them was to sell clothing at a very low price, as well as quilts and other things. The ladies' circles from the churches up north always sent boxes of used clothing as well as new articles. These were divided among the churches and each one then used them to help the needy. Eva Wedel found it easier to set aside Saturday to have the store open. She had a place near the garage where she kept the clothing. So on Saturday they came, one group after another, each trying to find the clothing they needed for themselves and their family. Eva Wedel used this time to witness to them about Christ. This work was continued by the missionaries that followed in later years.

I. THE MISSIONARIES AND PASTORS AT LA GRULLA

Ruben Wedel came from the Bessie (now Cordell), Oklahoma, Church and Eva Wiens came from the Bethel Church, Inman, Kansas. They met at Tabor College, married and went to Moody Bible Institute for a year. They felt the call of the Lord to work among Mexican Americans and wrote to the Mennonite Brethren Southern District Board. P.C. Hiebert came to Chicago, interviewed them and they were later accepted as workers for the Texas field. They arrived at Los Ebanos on September 14, 1945. They were ordained on November 3, 1946, at the Bessie Church. During the time they served at La Grulla they adopted two Mexican American boys, David and Darold. They served at La Grulla until May, 1956.

When the Wedels moved to pastor the Mennonite Brethren Church at Premont, Texas, Ruben attended college at Kingsville during their two years' stay. Then he began to teach in Alice, Texas, a year at Meade, Kansas, and back to the Valley in 1960. They lived in their own home in Pharr and both taught until they retired. Ruben taught and served in the emerging LAMB Conference on various boards, such as Administration, CYF, and Education. After a church opened at Pharr, they served there in various ways. During the summer months, however, they went to cook in youth camps in Colorado. In 1982, they requested their letter to join the Cordel, Oklahoma Church. Eva Wedel died April 28, 1984.

John and Daphyn (Delfina) Smith Savoia moved on May 31, 1956, to La Grulla, after serving a brief period at La Casita Church, to continue the work that had been started by the Ruben Wedels. The Savoias had been working in a mission in the Valley supporting themselves. He sold life insurance but they really longed to do mission work, so they gladly joined the Mennonite Brethren Southern District as missionaries. They served at La Grulla until 1959, when they left with four children, Debra, John, Timothy and Ruth. They went to the Mennonite Brethren Biblical Seminary at Fresno, California and, from there, went to Colombia as missionaries. They served for many years until Daphyn became too ill to continue. They returned to Hillsboro, Kansas, where she died, June 8, 1981. John remarried and went back to Colombia in 1983.

Alfredo and Ofelia Tagle came to La Grulla on August 15, 1959. Alfredo, a native of Lull, near Edinburg, and Ofelia, from Gomez Palacios, Durango, Mexico, are both graduates of the Rio Grande Bible Institute. Alfredo was ordained at Lull in May, 1960. For one year he served at Garciasville Church as well as at La Grulla. He first went to Garciasville to preach while La Grulla had their Sunday school. When he returned, he preached to the La Grulla congregation. The Tagles served at La Grulla until December 31, 1962, when they moved to Mexico to attend a Baptist seminary at Torreon. Upon returning, they stayed at Lull, where their fourth child, Moises, was born to be company to Benjamin, Elizabeth, and Ruth.

On August 15, 1964, the Tagles again returned to study in Torreon for one semester. They came back to Lull until they began to help the Alvin Neufelds in McAllen.

José and Graciela Lara and two children stayed at La Grulla church during summer, 1964. He taught the members that they were responsible to clean the church. José was teaching in El Faro School and was moved to take charge of the church at Los Ebanos.

Frank and Mary Jean Peterson Muñoz came to La Grulla Church in time for school in 1964 with three children, David, Jonathan and Debra. Although a native of Puerto Rico, he lost his parents at the age of four and was raised by an American couple and forgot the Spanish language. He met Mary Jean, a native of Nebraska, at Bible School in Dallas, where they both were students. Later at Dallas Theological Seminary, he met professor George Peters, a member of the Mennonite Brethren Conference Mission Board; from Peters he learned of the need for workers. The Muñoz family was accepted and given a year of Spanish language study at the Rio Grande Bible Institute. During that time, the family attended church at Lull. In fall, 1964, Frank began to teach at El Faro School and Mary Jean also helped and worked in the office until the spring, 1968. Sharon was born while they lived at La Grulla. They moved to El Faro grounds and still served at La Grulla for some time in 1969. Later they started an independent mission work at El Faro School.

Samuel Asencio, a student of Rio Grande Bible Institute, helped during summer, 1969. From the time that the Frank Muñoz family left the La Grulla Church, the congregation carried on the work with the help of German Contreras, Inocencio Garcia, and church members Rolando Mireles and Aniceto Zarate.

José Paulino, a student at RGBI, began to preach at La Grulla on February 6, 1972. Rolando Mireles went to pick him up each Sunday morning and returned him after the evening service. In summer, 1973, José Paulino married Alma Trevino, also a graduate of RGBI, who was working with Child Evangelism. José was a small man with a big voice. He served until he had to return to the Dominican Republic on February 18, 1974. During his absence, Alma lived in the parsonage and continued teaching others about Child Evangelism. Finally, after a year-and-a-half, José was able to return. He had been permitted to enter Mexico first, where he helped a Baptist church for some time at Camargo. There he was taken into custody by government agents for preaching without a license. Rolando Mireles, Alma Trevino and others went to check into the situation. After some days he was given papers to re-enter the United States and move back to his home at La Grulla. On November 30, 1977, they left to learn a skill to make a living.

From January to September the church was on its own and the preaching duties fell on Rolando Mireles and guest speakers. On Sunday nights Inocencio Garcia helped.

Then Paul J. Castillo came on September 1, 1977, from the Donna

Church, where he served as a student pastor. He married Eva Vellasco in December of 1981. She also had attended RGBI. The Castillos served until March 28, 1982. They later moved to California to pastor the Orosi Latin Mennonite Brethren Church.

The La Grulla Church was again without a pastor from March, 1982 to May, 1983. Rolando Mireles did the preaching most of the time. Carlos Calera held a meeting in La Grulla and recommended José Delgado. José J. and Dina Carrizales Delgado with daughter Dina Azucena came to La Grulla and moved into the new parsonage on June 1, 1983. José is a native of Mexico City. Later he attended the school on Walter Gomez' field in Montclova, Mexico. Dina Carrizales Delgado is a native of Montclova. He came to Montclova and there he was saved in one of the Walter Gomez missions. Jose later attended the Mexican Mission Ministries Seminary at Montclova. They had served a church in California before they moved into the new parsonage at La Grulla to take up the work begun before them. He went to work teaching a guitar class and promoted a better budget system in the church as well as visiting among the people.

CHAPTER 6

EL FARO SCHOOL

A. EARLY EVENTS THAT LED TO THE OPENING OF EL FARO SCHOOL

During the early forties, the missionaries and the congregations of Los Ebanos, Chihuahua, and La Grulla came to understand that if they wanted to bring up a new generation for the churches, they needed a Christian Day school. Instruction in the public schools of that day was poor because the children and teachers spoke mostly Spanish. The children of believers were sometimes called names, and occasionally abused. It cost something during those early years to be a real Christian. It even was hard to be a child of a believer.

One parent later expressed himself, saying, "In El Faro the children hear no bad words, so they grow up with a clean mind."

The burden of the missionaries and the churches to establish a school was presented to the Southern District Conference in 1946, just ten years after the work in South Texas had been accepted. The proposition was unanimously favored to proceed as soon as possible. A suitable piece of land was acquired February 2, 1948, near Highway 83, about a half mile east of Sullivan City, Texas. It lies just a few miles north of Los Ebanos.

B. THE BUILDINGS OF EL FARO SCHOOL

There was joy in the hearts of the missionaries and the congregations when actual work of clearing the land could finally begin. After removing the brush, they drilled a well and set up a windmill to have water. Local people came to do the clearing process. Everything except larger trees was removed.

At last the foundation was made and finally the first buff tile was laid. The missionaries, local people, and others from the north came to build the new school. Among these was the Albert Epp family, who stayed until all the work was done.

The new school had no name so the local board, Harry Neufeld, Henry Thomas, Ruben Wedel, and Ricardo Peña decided to allow each congregation to submit an idea. Ricardo Peña was going to Premont during weekends at that time, and he presented the cause to the congregation on Sunday night. There happened to be a visitor present and he suggested the name "El Faro." Ricardo liked it and submitted it to the board in the Valley. El Faro was chosen as the most fitting. The name means "The Lighthouse," and that is what the new school was dedicated to be.

By spring time, 1948, a Christian man, Glen Hamer, came to be the head mason and erect the El Faro School. The missionaries — Harry Neufeld, Henry Thomas, Ruben Wedel, Albert Epp — and Ricardo Peña toiled with the help of many others. They saw that the building could not be ready by September so the local board bought an old army barrack during the last weeks in August, moved it and arranged it for temporary classrooms. On November 18, 1948, the first class moved into the school and the Christmas program was given in the auditorium. The builders continued to work; it was January, 1949, when all the classes moved into the new building.

The school house, a buff tile modern structure, has a large classroom in the southwest corner (used for the first grade); an office and a smaller classroom on the west side; a hall all along the building; and two large classrooms with a moveable partition (which opens to form the auditorium). The original El Faro School was completed and dedicated on February 27, 1949.

Many had been waiting for the new school; there were 113 pupils in eight grades the first school year, 1948-1949. The first teachers were Miss Alvina Fast, the principal; Miss Viola Warkentin, from Meade, Kansas; Henry T. Esau from the Premont Mission; and Miss Susie Martin from Corn, Oklahoma. Henry T. Esau was released for the second semester and Miss Grace Unruh from Buhler, Kansas came to take his place.

Two new missions, Casita-Garciasville and La Joya, had come into the family, and there was a need for more space, including a gymnasium and auditorium. During 1951-53 a larger office, four classrooms and an auditorium were added to the school. The Fairview, Oklahoma, Mennonite Brethren Church was used by the Lord to provide the much-needed gymnasium in 1953. Men from the church brought a metal quonset and put it up in a short time. A stage and two small rooms were built across the north end. A special prayer room and a room for the school store were added later. A lower ceiling was made over the store and the entire south end of the building became storage space.

The four-classroom building, constructed in 1951, was connected by a covered walk along the south side. The west room was the school office and the next a classroom, then a larger one formed the library and study hall. The two east rooms were later used as a kitchen for the lunch program and a home economics class while the other became the science room. A wide walk ran north between the two buildings to the gymnasium, which was big enough for a basketball court and room for spectators.

The teachers boarded with the missionaries the first year before renting a brick house in Los Ebanos. By 1951 a three-apartment bricked modern teacherage was ready on the El Faro grounds. The back side had a large screened-in porch which served as a utility room for the teachers.

The old barrack was dismantled and the lumber was used to build the teacherage and a bus garage. More homes were needed when the Henry Boese's returned after four years of absence, so they built a small new house for them. The Albert Epps later moved this to Garciasville to make it into the parsonage. Then the so-called greenhouse was moved for the Raymond Vogts to live in. This later became an extra place for the typing classes and a sixth grade reading room. Then, in 1966, a government house was bought at Zapata and moved to El Faro. It was used for the lunch program until a classroom had a kitchen built in 1967. Alvin Neufeld was assigned to build cabinets and put in another sink. The original 1948 building was used for the elementary grades. The four rooms of 1951 were used for the upper grades and later also for high school.

C. HOW EL FARO SCHOOL OPERATED

From the beginning, the El Faro School committee and the Home Missions Board worked in harmony to sustain it and make it a tool of evangelism and follow-up work among Mennonite Brethren Mexican Americans in South Texas. It was totally supported by the Southern District Conference (because it was one arm of its missions) but fees were soon charged for each pupil. By 1965, $5.00 a month was expected for the first child and $3.00 for each additional one of the same family. All this helped, but it could not support the school.

The first local school board was comprised of Harry Neufeld, Henry Thomas, Ruben Wedel and Ricardo Peña.

The GLEAM, the first annual of El Faro, was published in 1951 and dedicated to Harry Neufeld, the pioneer missionary of Mennonite Brethren in South Texas. It tells of his faithful and untiring devotion to his calling that made El Faro and four mission stations possible.

The fourth station, Premont, belonged to the Southern District Mission Program but was too far away to fully join in with El Faro. The Premont Mennonite Brethren Church helped the school when possible but could not send any pupils to the Valley.

The Southern District Mennonite Brethren Conference elected a committee to oversee its home missions. In 1948 it consisted of three ministers: Orlando Harms, Elmo Warkentin and Abe W. Epp. These three did much for El Faro and they served for years in different offices. In 1951 Harms was the chairman; Warkentin, secretary; and A.W. Epp, treasurer.

During the next five years many changes took place in the local as well as in the Southern District Committees. By 1957 the Home Mission Committee had become the Home Mission Board and only A.W. Epp was still serving. The others were ministers of different churches: Loyal Funk, Ervin Adrian (secretary), Reuben Baerg (chairman), E.C. Ollenburger, B.W. Vogt, and J.J. Gerbrandt.

The local committee was called the Board of Education with Ricardo Peña as chairman. The others were Candelario Gutierrez, Raymond Vogt (teacher and secretary), Inocencio Garcia (missionary), Albert Epp (teacher), and John Savoia (missionary).

The GLEAM of 1957 tells of A.W. Epp of Fairview, Oklahoma, who had served eighteen years on the Southern District Home Missions Board. It says that, "Rev. Epp had been instrumental in the beginning and expansion of our school. Often he had come to South Texas personally to help in constructing new buildings and planning the future of El Faro School. His untiring service for the cause of missions is an inspiration to students and faculty."

In 1964, the 15th anniversary of El Faro School, the GLEAM shows all new board members of the Home Mission Committee of the Southern District — William Neufeld, Raymond Vogt, David Plett, Abe Klassen and J.R. Bergman. The local school board was composed of all Mexican Americans — Leonel Saenz, Ricardo Peña (pastor), Juan Noyola, Antonio Garcia, and Abelardo Mireles, in addition to the superintendent, Daniel Wirsche — showing the shift away from the pastors. By this time, the young LAMB Conference was composed of the following churches: Casita-Garciasville, La Grulla, Los Ebanos, La Joya, Chihuahua, Mission, a future group in McAllen, and Lull, north of Edinburg. All of these congregations had a part in the support of El Faro.

Since its beginning in 1963, the Latin American Mennonite Brethren (LAMB) Conference elected its own Educational Board. The Southern District was still in charge of the greater part of the school's support and its activity through the Texas Commission, consisting of Raymond Vogt and Edwin Karber.

The 1966 GLEAM was dedicated to Daniel Wirsche. It says, "He has faithfully served his Lord, laboring as superintendent and teacher of El Faro School. His hard and faithful work is deeply appreciated by the students and faculty."

The next LAMB Conference elected H.T. Esau and Jonas Ybarra to replace Abelardo Mireles and Juan Noyola. By 1964 Alfredo Tagle and Anselmo Salinas came into the scene. Ricardo Peña had stayed on the board since its beginning in 1948, serving as secretary and as chairman.

By 1964 the zeal and the interest of the Southern District had shifted, with people believing that the work in Texas was old enough to stand on its own feet. The closing note of information sent concerning El Faro says: "We believe these proposed guidelines reflect neither defeat, nor a retraction, but a redirection to give new emphasis to evangelism and church building."

The support which had come from the Southern district was gradually phased out and the small Conference, LAMB in the Valley, was unable to keep El Faro. So, with sorrow, the conference-related activities had to move out. During the last year, 1968-1969, there was only a grade school and Frank Muñoz taught the high school students in his own building, using some El Faro equipment. He was later able to buy the El Faro plant in 1973, using the place ever since. For a number of years there was a government-run pre-school in the elementary building. The library is used by a group that meets there for worship.

D. THE CURRICULUM OF EL FARO SCHOOL

The El Faro curriculum met Texas requirements, plus Bible instruction. Problems were handled in a Christ-like manner. Children were taught to speak good English and use of foul language was not permitted. When students argued or fought, they were asked to go pray about the matter and forgive each other. Corporal punishment was administered as a last resort by the principal, with a witness present.

El Faro used Texas state-adopted texts, although there were less elective courses offered in high school because of a shortage of teachers and equipment. The shortage, however, was offset by Bible teaching and Christian living exemplified by the teachers.

The older students had prayer meetings (girls and boys separated). They taught Spanish as a foreign language credit and, while Daniel Wirsche was teaching, he taught a course in German, which was much enjoyed.

All pupils who entered grade nine in 1962 were required to complete at least sixteen units plus two units of physical and health education, besides Bible, to graduate. Among the electives were Homemaking, Mechanical Drawing, Christian Music, Speech and Typing. El Faro had a good choir that frequently visited churches. They learned to read music, something that was new in the churches where parts were sung by ear. El Faro stimulated a greater appreciation for music, especially in those churches who had members in the choir. Some also learned to play piano, and so helped their churches.

The pupils and students of El Faro were well up with those of the public schools. Some were way ahead of the classes to which they transferred after El Faro closed. In most cases, they had a better English and were better in other subjects as well. El Faro teachers were there to teach both subject matter and build their students' character.

E. ACTIVITIES OF EL FARO SCHOOL

The parents of El Faro students had a Parent Teacher Association which met at the school regularly. They prayed and worked to raise money for its support. The P.T.A. was led by three parents and two teachers.

El Faro put out a yearbook six times; it was produced by students, with teachers as sponsors. The annual, named the GLEAM, showed light coming from the Lighthouse. The first issue, in May, 1951, was historical and gave a brief story of the four churches of that time and showed the development of the first building on a plot of four acres of land. It was dedicated to Harry Neufeld, the first missionary. The next issue, published in 1957, tells that they had a superintendent and a principal because four more classrooms and a gymnasium had been added. It was dedicated to A.W. Epp of Fairview, Oklahoma, and showed the first high school graduating class of Gordon Neufeld, Eraclio Villarreal, Belsa Gutierrez, and Juanita Cortez. These seniors had a Sneak Day and a Senior Picnic.

The third annual, published in 1964, for the fifteenth anniversary of El Faro, gives a picture history of the barrack, the first place where classes met in 1948, the first student body, first teachers, H.T. Esau, Viola Warkentin, Alvina Fast (principal), Susie Martin, and Grace Unruh, second semester, and the first school board, Ruben Wedel, Harry Neufeld, Henry Thomas, and Ricardo Peña. The school buildings and the teacherage are also pictured. It also gives a complete list of all teachers who had taught in El Faro up to 1964.

Just two years later, in 1966, another GLEAM came out. This one was dedicated to Daniel Wirsche.

The 1967-1968 GLEAM was the last one, published just one year before the school was closed. A celebration of twenty years (1948-1968), its motto was: "Jesus Christ, the same yesterday, today, and forever" (Hebrews 13:8). It was dedicated to all the teachers who taught at El Faro during the years, with love and devotion to their Lord and the task. This book has a picture of the local school board elected by the LAMB Conference.

On May 17, 1968, the largest class of eight high school seniors graduated and received their diplomas from the chairman of the board, H.T. Esau.

For some time during the fifties, El Faro teachers and students published a paper of six legal-sized sheets which gave news of the churches and the school. It was named EL FARO. These preserved much material of interest.

Later, during the sixties, the faculty of El Faro mimeographed THE BEACON for some time, which also published news about the teachers and needs of El Faro.

Music was a great part of the life of El Faro School. Songs and music is a part of the Mexican way of life. In El Faro they sang in every age group. They had a select choir for church programs. They had music clubs for children's choir, one for junior and senior high school, and another for the sixth grade. In 1966, Annie Dyck was the pianist and Mrs. Mary Jean Muñoz was piano teacher. Mrs. Alvina Boese also directed various musical groups during her long stay at El Faro. There was a trio that went to sing at the Southern District Conference in 1963. This training in music carried over into the churches. A knowledge of music resulted in better choirs and singing. The students were able to learn songs from books and did not have to rely only on hearing them from others.

Every year there were special revival meetings for each group level. Yolanda Villarreal, a Child Evangelism teacher, often came to present the gospel to the younger children, as well as to others. During the 1965-66 school year, Wilfred Thiessen from the Rio Grande Bible Institute was the evangelist for the older students. Zeral Brown served a week one year.

During those weeks the claims of Christ were especially stressed and made clear. Children and older ones made professions of faith while others dedicated their lives to the Lord to live for Him in whatever way He would lead them.

Besides an hour of daily Bible studies and prayer for all the grades, for a few years they also had Bible quiz times. The winners went on Saturday nights to compete for the award at Youth for Christ meetings held in city school auditoriums. El Faro School stood up well against the youth of Valley churches.

For a period there were various clubs, such as English and Bible memorization. Students worked to become more fluent in language and also hide the Word in their hearts. In 1966 the girls had a basketball team that went to play other schools such as Weslaco, La Joya, Sharyland and Raymondville.

Besides all else, there was always something going on in the gymnasium or on the school yard for physical education classes or just sport for fun.

After the school had a regular kitchen, girls learned to bake cakes, pies, rolls, and much more by the excellent teaching of Mrs. Alvina Boese. These cooking skills are still in use in the homes of church members.

Alvina Boese also taught craft classes in the eighth grade during 1966. The students painted Spanish plaques which they prized very much.

Each year El Faro prepared a big Christmas program for parents and friends. By 1954 they used the auditorium that held hundreds of people. Many who never went to the churches would come to the programs, and heard the gospel in word and song. The programs were well prepared and interesting. There was also fun for the children at the annual Christmas party. They got to break a real piñata.

There were recreational activities all year but a special event was the Field Day. That time the winners in races, various kinds of jumping, and other athletic exercises were determined. This was a time of fun as well as real work, but there was joy for those who won awards.

F. THE TEACHERS OF EL FARO SCHOOL DURING TWENTY-ONE YEARS

To the teachers, students, pupils, and parents, El Faro was very dear because it was the only service to the Lord all the churches held in common. To them it was clear the Lord raised up El Faro and guided it through problems, one upon another, but He always gave victory for all to see "What God has done."

The teachers who came to El Faro gave the best of their lives to teach children and present Christ to them in their daily living with great devotion. These teachers had their own prayer meetings to ask for God's help.

In twenty-one years, around forty different persons taught in El Faro, not counting the missionaries, who at times had to help out, or the teacher aids and secretaries.

(1) Teachers Who Served El Faro Ten or More Years:

Alvina Fast (Mrs. Henry Boese) taught first grade and was the first principal from 1948 to 1951. While the three teachers (Miss Fast, Miss Vogt and Miss Martin) lived in a rented teacherage in Los Ebanos, Alvina Fast and Henry Boese were married and they moved to a smaller house in the village. The Boese's left to teach at the mission school at Indianoma, Oklahoma. From there they moved to San Jose, California.

In 1955 Henry and Alvina Boese returned to El Faro with two small children, Lawanna and Paul. They stayed until 1968, the twentieth year of El Faro. She taught first grade, English for grades 7, 8, 9, music, homemaking, crafts, and typing. In grade school or high school, wherever there was a need, she filled the place. For years they lived in the west apartment of the teacherage. They also taught in summer Bible schools where needed. In the spring of 1968 they moved to San Jose, California where she taught and Henry worked until they retired.

Ruth Wiens was in Tabor College when she heard about El Faro School through Priscilla Fast, a sister of Alvina Boese. Since she wanted to teach in a Christian school, she contacted El Faro and came to teach in 1954. Ruth was principal of the elementary school from 1962-69 and taught the third grade except 1965-1966, in which she took the first grade. During the last year of the school, she also taught eighth grade mathematics. Ruth Wiens stayed in El Faro and taught for fifteen years. She helped in the churches of La Grulla, La Casita, and Chihuahua until it was merged with La Joya. One year she helped in the outreach at La Homa and then at La Joya after the merger. Ruth and her sister Mariana lived in the east apartment of the teacherage. When El Faro closed, the sisters both went to Rio Grande Bible Institute to study Spanish. From there they went to teach in a missionary children's school and helped in a Spanish church in Guadalajara, Mexico. They later moved to Salem, Oregon.

Mariana Wiens learned to know Eleanor Vogt from Premont, Texas, while in Tabor College. Vogt began to teach in El Faro after she graduated in 1949. Ruth also influenced Mariana. At Grace Bible Institute, and in her own church at Mountain Lake, Minnesota, she heard Walter Gomez report and show pictures of the work in the Valley. The Lord led Mariana to El Faro in 1956. She generally taught the fourth grade, except in 1956-66, when she also had the third grade. She did a great deal of the bookkeeping for the school and ran the school store. Mariana Wiens gave thirteen years of her life to El Faro.

She helped at the churches of Los Ebanos and at Mission in the mornings and at Chihuahua in the evenings.

The Albert Epps came to help build the elementary school in 1948, before returning to Tabor College so that he could finish his education. Albert and Emily Epp, along with Gloria, Mary Lou, and Barbara, moved to El Faro in 1951. At first he was the coach and taught mathematics, science and Bible. In 1957 he became superintendent of the school and served in that capacity until 1961. Mrs. Epp also helped at school. In 1957 she was study hall supervisor. The Epps lived in the teacherage until they moved to Garciasville. They worked at the Casita-Garciasville Church for ten years. When the churches became independent, they moved to Corn, Oklahoma in August, 1961 to teach at the Academy. They left their hearts in the Valley. Emily Epp died in July of 1980. Albert Epp is remarried and lives in Corn, Oklahoma.

Elizabeth Adrian came in 1951 and taught the first grade for ten years. She didn't know Spanish when she came; yet, somehow, with drawings and motions, taught the children English. She was loved by her little ones and imparted more than just knowledge to them. There was always a group who found it too difficult to learn enough English to read, so there were two classes to teach.

For part of this time Elizabeth Adrian was also principal of the school. When the teacherage was ready, she and Susie Martin moved into the small middle apartment. The two lived together for four years, and after that Adrian lived alone.

As did the other teachers, Adrian helped teach Vacation Bible school in the churches. One year she came to Premont to teach the pre-schoolers. It was a very large class but, with some help, she managed.

In 1961 she moved back to her family home to live with her sisters at Hillsboro, Kansas. She began to work at the hospital to help in time of retirement. She died on July 27, 1973.

(2) Teachers Who Taught at El Faro Five or More Years:

Susie Martin left Corn, Oklahoma, in May, 1948 to go help in the Henry Thomas home, so Ruth could be free to teach more women's classes. El Faro was opened and there were not enough teachers so Susie was drafted for part-time and then full-time teaching. During the eight years she taught mostly second, third, and fourth grades. The first year she lived with the Thomas' at Abram. The second year she lived with Alvina Fast and Eleanor Vogt in a large apartment house in Los Ebanos, which belonged to the Federico Peña family. The Harold Warkentins lived in the other side. Then, when the teacherage was finished in 1951, Susie and Elizabeth Adrian moved into the small middle apartment. In 1954, Susie, together with Ruth Wiens and Olga Guerra, moved to the east apartment vacated by the Harold Warkentins.

In 1956 Susie Martin left to go work for Back to the Bible Broadcast, staying there until she retired. In 1982 she married missionary Henry Thomas and lives in Soquel, California.

Daniel A. Wirsche of Saskatchewan, Canada, graduated from Tabor College and also studied at Fresno, California State and Emporia (Kansas) State Colleges. Daniel and Elsie Wirsche spent ten years in Colombia with Mennonite Brethren Missions and also served in Mexico. He taught two years at El Faro before becoming Superintendent in 1962. He taught until 1966. After that both he and Elsie helped out with teaching where needed. They resigned mid-year 1966 to prepare to go back to South America. Together with Donald, their youngest son, they left for Montevideo, Uruguay in March, 1968. The Wirsches served in the Rio Grande Valley from January, 1960 to March, 1968. Since then, they have been in Uruguay and Mexico, serving in the mission and in Montevideo. They returned January, 1985 to pastor the La Joya church.

Eleanor Vogt from the Mennonite Brethren Church at Premont came to teach at El Faro in September, 1949. She was a graduate of Tabor College and lived in the rented teacherage in Los Ebanos with Susie Martin and Alvina Fast. During 1951 she taught second and third grades, and taught until 1954. She married Dan Petker and together they worked in Mexico as missionaries for a few years and then both taught in Fresno, California.

Harold B. and Rosena Loewen Warkentin came in 1949. He taught upper grades; in 1951 he had the sixth, seventh, and eighth grades. After Alvina Boese left in 1951, he became principal. The Warkentins helped Ricardo Peña teaching Sunday school and conducting services at Casita, a new work. They lived in the rented teacherage in Los Ebanos until the new one was finished on El Faro grounds. They moved into the east apartment and lived there until 1954, and later moved away to teach in other Christian schools.

David Fast from the Hooker (Oklahoma) Mennonite Brethren Church (now Adams), felt the call to mission work and came to the Valley to finish his education at Pan American University in Edinburg, Texas. He began to teach in El Faro in 1962. David Fast lived at Garciasville parsonage and taught the fifth and sixth grades in El Faro. He worked in the church and also was a bus driver. He married Martha Kroeker, a missionary working in Colombia; she also taught in El Faro in 1964. They left with a son, Paul, in 1966 and went to work for the Gospel Missionary Union in Panama.

(3) Teachers Who Taught at El Faro for Less Than Five Years:

Belsa Gutierrez was the first El Faro student to teach others in the school she loved. She had attended Tabor College in Hillsboro, Kansas — one of the first of the Latin students to do so. A native of the La Grulla Church, she taught the second grade for three years, during 1962 to 1965. Then, the last year, in 1969, when Belsa G. Villarreal came to finish the first grade left vacant by a resignation, she taught three-and-a-half years at El Faro. She lives near the La Grulla water tower and is active in the church.

Ray Vogt, from the Premont Mennonite Brethren Church, came to El Faro as principal in 1953 and stayed until 1957. The teacherage was occupied, so a house was moved in for the Vogt's. This was the first time a brother and sister taught at El Faro together for two years. They left to take a pastorate of the new Mennonite Brethren Church at Tulsa, Oklahoma, in 1957.

Elaine Schroeder of the Buhler, Kansas, Mennonite Brethren Church, came to El Faro to teach first grade after Miss Adrian left in 1961. Elaine, a Christian Service worker, stayed on and later taught sixth grade Bible and sixth through tenth grade science classes in El Faro. She left in spring, 1965, to do graduate work in Library Science.

Connie Savoia came from the east to El Faro in fall, 1957, and lived with her brother John and family in La Grulla. She taught in the grade school for two years until May, 1959. She also helped in the La Grulla church.

Geneva Kime (Mrs. Daniel Kime) and family — Kennert, Dannie, and Alane — moved to La Joya, where they took care of the church and where she taught first grade for two years. They also lived a year at Lull helping the church with Alvin Neufeld. The Kimes left in 1965 to go to Panama to serve as missionaries. Geneva has been teaching missionary children in a Mission school for many years.

Olga Guerra came from the Garciasville Church and taught in El Faro from 1954 to 1956. She married and moved to Rio Grande City.

José Lara of Mexico had been educated at Bob Jones University, Greenville, South Carolina. He taught sixth, seventh, ninth and tenth grade Bible and eighth grade mathematics and Spanish. José and his wife, Graciela, and their children Jorge and Jaime lived in the house Harry Neufeld built in Los Ebanos. They took care of the church and taught the members. They left in 1965 to do mission work in Mexico.

Mrs. Ruth Stewart, formerly librarian at the Rio Grande Bible Institute, came to El Faro to teach first grade in 1965. She later taught shorthand and typing in the high school. In May, 1967, she left El Faro to help in a Christian school at Roma, Texas.

Frank Muñoz, a native of Puerto Rico and a graduate of Dallas Theological Seminary, came to the Rio Grande Bible Institute to study Spanish. The family was assigned to attend church at Lull. In 1964 they moved to La Grulla Church with children David, Jonathan and Debra (Sharon was born later). Frank taught Bible, Economics, English Literature and seventh and eighth grade History during 1963-64 and taught and served as superintendent from 1966-68. Mary Jean taught piano and also worked in the office. He bought El Faro School in May, 1973, and has lived near it since.

Wilma Smith came from the Christian school at La Feria, Texas, and was loaned to El Faro by her mission. During 1965-66 she taught seventh to tenth grade science. She taught two years and lived on the campus.

Frieda Buller from Enid, Oklahoma, came for the 1966-67 school year and taught second grade. She lived on the campus and stayed to the end of the last school year. She taught three years and returned home and later went to teach together with Ruth and Mariana Wiens in the Missionary Children School at Guadalajara, Mexico.

Tim Kliewer graduated from Tabor College in 1961, married Myrna Nickel and together they came to El Faro as newlyweds so that he could perform alternative service as a Christian Service worker. He taught and drove the bus; for the second semester of 1964, Myrna finished the school year for Donna Beth Wiebe. Tim taught two years in El Faro. They moved to California where she took up nurses training and he received his Masters Degree from Mennonite Brethren Biblical Seminary at Fresno, California.

Nilda Cantu, one of the El Faro pupils from the La Grulla Church, took the second grade left vacant by Belsa Gutierrez in September, 1965 and taught two years.

Max Bulsterbaum lived in Edinburg, Texas, attending Pan American University while his wife taught in high school. He came to El Faro in fall, 1967, and taught fifth and sixth grades until 1969 when the school closed. He left Edinburg to teach in the Corpus Christi area.

Mrs. Catherine Peterson Crandall, a sister of Mrs. Frank Muñoz, came to teach the first grade in 1967 and taught for two years. She lived on campus.

(4) Teachers Who Taught at El Faro One Year or Less:

Henry T. Esau was one of the four teachers who began El Faro in 1948, teaching seventh and eighth grades in the barrack for the first semester before returning to the mission at Premont. He stayed at Henry Thomas' home and returned home every Friday after school.

Grace Unruh, from Buhler, Kansas, came to teach first grade in 1949 so Alvina Fast could take Henry Esau's classes. Grace stayed with the Harry Neufelds.

Dolores Balzer of Bingham Lake, Minnesota, taught in El Faro 1953-54, returning to her home state to teach after one year. She roomed with the Harold Warkentins and ate with Susie Martin and Elizabeth Adrian.

Leonel Saenz came from the Casita-Garciasville Church and taught 1956-57 in El Faro. He has since acquired a Masters Degree, lives in Garciasville, and teaches in La Grulla.

Alpha Guerra of Garciasville taught 1959-60.

Dan Petker taught in El Faro 1960-61. He married Eleanor Vogt of Premont, Texas, and they served as missionaries in Monterrey, Mexico, and later both taught in Fresno, California.

Paul Wiebe and Donna Beth came to El Faro in 1961, and he served as superintendent for one year.

Anna Enns, a Mennonite Brethren missionary from the Belgian Congo (Zaire), taught one year 1962-63. She went to another mission in Nigeria.

Mrs. Margery Erlandson came from the Rio Grande Language School and taught the first grade in fall, 1968. Belsa G. Villarreal finished the year for her.

Yolanda Villarreal, a missionary Child Evangelism teacher,

helped out from time to time. She filled several places during the last year of El Faro.

Annie Dyck, who lived with Yolanda, was also drafted to fill needs in the school. Since both Annie and Yolanda were in charge of the La Joya Church and also attended Pan American University, they helped out in El Faro as their schedules permitted.

Alfred Tagle also taught Bible during the last year of El Faro School.

Through the years other missionaries helped when and where needed as they could. Ofelia Tagle taught Spanish in 1967-68.

G. THE NON-TEACHING STAFF OF EL FARO

Henry Boese lived at El Faro, serving as head custodian and maintenance man; he also often drove a bus, and during the years, also taught some classes. Throughout the school year he received help for the cleaning work. During the summer he undertook the repair.

Many of the missionaries and teachers drove buses. Two, and sometimes four, vehicles were going in different directions to bring in pupils. Some of the students, laymen, pastors and teachers who drove the buses were Gordon Neufeld, Wesley Wirsche, Juan Noyola, José Lara, and David Fast. Inocencio Garcia was the bus mechanic for years.

After the teaching load became too heavy (because the school could no longer afford the needed teachers) they doubled up so those teachers who had been doing book work on the side could give this responsibility to secretaries hired for the job. Mrs. Mary Jean Munoz, the principal's wife, did the office work during part of 1967. Zita Noyola from Abram and the Chihuahua Church served from 1965-66 and Juanita Noyola, a sister to Zita, served from 1966-67. Maria Luisa Peña from Los Ebanos worked 1967-68, and Olivia, another sister to Zita, worked the last year, 1968-69.

H. THE KITCHEN STAFF AND THE LUNCH PROGRAM

Even though it was clear to the El Faro School board and the teachers that the time would come when all support would be withdrawn, they kept adding improvements to El Faro to the last.

In 1965 the school received government aid and provided milk for the children at lunch time. More government aid later allowed the school to provide a complete hot lunch program, which began in 1965-66. Mrs. Consuelo Villarreal from Abram was the first cook, with Mrs. Lucia Salinas joining her later. In spring, when many left to work in northern states, Mrs. Villarreal did the cooking work alone. The girls from the upper grades and high school helped serve food and wash dishes.

The lunch program was served from a kitchen with all the needed equipment; it also served as a classroom to teach homemaking to girls.

Some children received free lunches from aid given to El Faro through schools in Hidalgo and Starr Counties (from where the children came). Others paid a small sum. The 1968 annual shows Alicia Gonzales as head cook and Lucia Salinas as assistant; both served for two years. In 1967-68 Alicia, from Mission, came to El Faro in the bus that gathered children from that area. Lucia first lived in the parsonage at Garciasville but later lived at La Joya, where her husband was the pastor of the Mennonite Brethren Church. Both cooks served during the last year of El Faro.

I. THE LASTING RESULTS OF EL FARO SCHOOL

El Faro School came into existence to bring up and educate a new generation of Christians, grounded in Bible knowledge. This was accomplished through consistent Bible training and Christian living by the faculty and all who had a part in serving at El Faro during twenty-one years.

The period of Bible study each day is still a vivid memory in the minds of those pupils who attended El Faro. Some say it was the best part of the day.

El Faro reached children whose parents did not attend any of the local mission churches; hundreds of people had an opportunity to see the gospel in action. Many received the Lord as students and later became parents who taught Christian living to their children. Many of the workers in the present churches are former El Faro students.

Another blessing of El Faro for the churches is that many learned to read music, while others learned to play the piano. The many choruses the children learned remain a part of them through life. El Faro sowed the Word of God in hearts of children and was a witness of evangelical Christianity left by the example of excellent dedicated Christian teachers.

There were only four twelfth grade graduating classes in El Faro, in 1957, 1964, 1966 and 1968. All six members of the class of 1968 spent all twelve years in El Faro. A good number of El Faro students have attended college and entered professions. Two El Faro students returned to teach in El Faro, four became secretaries and one was a cook. By 1968, four former students served on Conference boards with others joining later. El Faro students have become pastors, deacons, Sunday school teachers, youth leaders, piano players and workers among children and women's circles.

This and much more is what God has done in and through El Faro, a true light that shone in a world of darkness.

CHAPTER 7

THE MENNONITE BRETHREN MISSION AT PREMONT, TEXAS

A. EARLY ATTEMPTS TO EVANGELIZE THE PREMONT AREA

The Presbyterians had services in Premont among the Spanish-speaking people for some time, but only two families were left by 1948. Next came an (Old) Mennonite couple, Mr. and Mrs. A.H. Kauffman, who worked in the area. After some years they moved to a building and conducted services whenever they came to Premont. They had baptized one family before deciding to move to Matthies. The Mennonite Mission offered the little chapel at Premont to the Mennonite Brethren, who, through the Sunday school work of the Henry Andres and P.E. Penner, had presented the gospel. The people seemed friendly enough, coming to services and making professions of faith, but were unwilling to be baptized.

The Mennonite Brethren at Premont bought the little chapel in 1946 and began to conduct services; the Southern District accepted it at the 1946 Conference. Meanwhile, B.W. Vogt and teachers, Alvina Fast and Martha Foote from the church took care of regular services. The members at Premont prayed for full-time workers; God answered their prayers when B.W. Vogt met the H.T. Esaus at a Tabor College commencement. He said to himself, "I have found my workers."

The call was unexpected, but the Lord put a desire in the hearts of Henry, Anna and son Kenneth Esau. They spent their 1947 summer vacation working on the mission fields at Post Oak and Lawton City Mission in Oklahoma and in South Texas along the Rio Grande. They stopped at Premont, visited with friends they knew, and again were challenged to take over the work.

They decided to meet the challenge, sold their home, gave up teaching and began work at Premont on half salary from the Southern District Mission Board. (Premont does not belong to the Valley proper, but is included in this record because it was a part of the Mennonite Brethren Southern District work from 1946-60).

B. THE FIELD OF PREMONT

Premont lies one hundred miles north of the Rio Grande River on Highway 281. Ricardo Peña from Los Ebanos was sent to serve on weekends at the little Premont chapel in 1947, coming for over a year until the Esaus took over the work. Tanguma, a Presbyterian, knew everyone and took Ricardo and the Esaus to people open to the gospel. They invited these people to the services.

Premont is similar to cities in the Valley, yet in some respects it is different. There are wealthy Mexican American land owners who employ many people; the result is that fewer migrate to follow crops, as is the case in the Valley. Many more Mexican Americans understood and spoke English than in the Lower Valley.

C. THE PREMONT STATION

Henry T. and Anna Hiebert Esau and Kenneth, a high school freshman, reached Premont on a very hot day, June 10, 1948 and were welcomed by the Premont Mennonite Brethren Church. They lived with the Henry Andres in Falfurias for two weeks before buying a house on the west side that had only two enclosed rooms. They worked on it until school started, when Henry was needed as seventh and eighth grade teacher. He went to stay for the week at the Henry Thomases while Anna and Kenneth took care of the work at home. Ricardo Peña came home with Henry each Friday after school and met people gathered for a service. Anna and Kenneth had gathered the people in the old Canosa, a silver-topped panel truck which had been sent to Premont from the Valley. They sang until the two could reach Premont to conduct the service.

The old mission was on only a 25-foot lot and the neighbors were very near. They played their radio as loud as possible in order to drown out the service.

The house the Esaus bought on the west side of Premont was far from ready for the winter, so Albert Epp and Ricardo Peña came to help for a long weekend. The stove was set up and sheetrock put on the walls. In January Henry was released from El Faro and they worked to finish the house. The house was later sold to help pay for the better home on the east side. Ricardo began to teach Spanish to the Esaus on weekends; they later found a teacher in Falfurias who helped them to learn to read and speak.

About a year after the Esaus arrived a very nice large tract of land was bought; the Esaus purchased five lots for their house and the Conference paid for six 25-foot lots for the chapel.

Henry and Kenneth had taken down an old store in western Kansas; a big truck owned by Arnie Penner of Inman, Kansas, moved it from Long Island, Kansas, to Premont. The lumber was piled up in a big neat stack in the back yard of the house on the west side of town. Some of it went into finishing the first house and the rest was later used for the house and barn on the east side.

In 1950 they built a chapel with a wing for two Sunday school classes just west of the house. It later received a sign, "The Chapel of the Lord," to show to all going by that this house belonged to God.

For two years they used the chapel, although it was unfinished on the inside. Henry bought a furnace and set it up along the east wall;

it always kept the chapel warm even during cold spells.

In October, 1952, the Esaus began to finish the inside of the chapel. It was ready for the dedication, December 26, 1952. Every seat was taken by local people and the guests from the various stations of the Valley for the morning dedication service. Abe W. Epp from Fairview, Oklahoma, treasurer of the Board of Home Missions, spoke about faithfulness and J.P. Kliewer delivered the dedicatory address. The Lord's prayer was sung by Ricardo Zapata, and prayers of dedication were offered by the brethren A.W. Epp, Harry Neufeld and H.T. Esau.

Following a noon meal, all went to the house and dedicated it to the Lord. In the afternoon a children's story was presented by Yolanda Villarreal and three short messages were given between musical numbers. Ricardo Peña told of early experiences in Premont and J.N.C. Hiebert from Tabor College described the Old and the New Song in India. Albert Epp from El Faro spoke on the greatest gift. The offering was presented to El Faro School.

Years later a second house was built just east of the missionary home. Abe and Sarah Esau, brother and sister to Henry, came to live with them. Abe kept the grass cut and the church in order. For a year the four ate together until the second house could be finished. This house later was moved and rebuilt at Edinburg, Texas, providing a home for them. In its study Anna wrote the Bible course, "Search the Scriptures," in Spanish. All have been translated into English.

D. WORK AMONG THE CHILDREN, YOUTH AND ADULTS AT PREMONT

It was difficult to have three Sunday school classes in the little chapel. Ricardo Peña taught the adults, Henry Esau the young people, and Anna the children. It was a relief to have a room for each class after the house was built; two more Sunday school rooms were later added to the bus garage to give more room for the large classes. It was also a great help when Victor and Sara Ann Flaming came to help teach. Others who helped teach were Arthur and Verda May Byerly, Bill and Doris Goertz and Sarah Esau.

The two week Bible school was a great event in Premont. Alvina Fast and Susie Martin from El Faro came to help teach the first year. Others who helped teach through the years were Elizabeth Adrian, Juanita Cortez and Lucia Garcia.

To draw older girls, Anna Esau had a cookie baking class in the afternoons. They baked enough for a treat for each child the next day. On the last day of Bible school, they had a picnic at noon. The children ate all the watermelon they could hold.

The Bible school each year was a great attraction because many children heard they would get to paint plaques. Those Bible verses went up on the walls of homes where parents would not permit the Bible to enter. The plaques, mostly in Spanish, were touched up and varnished. One year they made, "The blood of Jesus Christ cleanseth

us from all sin," in Spanish. One girl later came to Mrs. Esau and said,
"I have it hanging just above the door and I always read it and now I
believe it!" One year some two hundred children came to Bible school.
Anna put varnish on five hundred pieces that had been painted that
year.

The Esaus worked on the plaques after Bible school until all were
ready. Then they sorted them according to families and went to visit
each home. The doors were open wide to get their plaques, and the
adults listened to some Bible verses and a prayer.

During 1952-56, Kenneth recruited teachers from Tabor College
to serve in Bible School, permitting the young people of the mission
who taught on Sundays and on Wednesdays to also attend a class. The
Bible school teachers lived and ate at the Esaus.

Each year after practicing for the Christmas program was over,
spring work began. It took much time and work to design the Spanish
plaques for each year and then make all the casts for the children who
would attend the Bible school.

On Good Friday a picnic was held. Henry took a bus load of children to a pasture to play games while the mothers stayed at church
to fix a big meal. Those who went out to play returned hungry and
ready to eat. In the afternoon there was a special service with some
invited guests; one year Victor Ovando, an ex-priest from Nicaragua,
was the speaker and three adults professed salvation. Since there was
no school on Good Friday, many came to the picnic, including adults.
The people of Premont celebrated Saturday as "Sabado de Gloria"
(Sabbath of Glory). That is the end of Lent and at midnight they
danced the Lord out of the grave and their vows were ended. In Premont at that time, very few Mexican Americans went to church on Easter Sunday. That was family day for picnics.

On Mother's Day there was another celebration. The children
brought special numbers and the young people sang special Mother's
Day songs. Each mother received a corsage and some received a prize.

Anna devoted much time to children's work. On Mondays the
younger girls came for club, with the older ones coming on Tuesdays.
They sang, listened to a Bible lesson and did some craft project. They
earned badges for some work assigned by the Pioneer Girls Club.

The Esaus continued the Friday night adult Bible classes in the
homes of various families. The adults studied illustrated lessons written on 36 by 24 inch sheets that the Herwanna Chapter, Buhler, Kansas, made for the mission. These lessons formed the basis from which
the eleven books "Escrudinad Las Escrituras" (Search the Scriptures)
were later written.

On Wednesday night there was a regular Bible school with classes
for all ages.

During the summer time there were no clubs because some children went to pick cotton. Two families still had no cars, so Henry Esau
took them to work in the morning and went to take them home for a
rest until towards evening when they went out again.

Summer time was also an opportunity to keep the Sunday school children and young people reading books from the church library. There was a nice collection of good books for them to read. The Esaus later heard that the teachers in Premont schools spotted those who had read all summer.

E. WORK FOR PEOPLE IN PREMONT

The mission circles in the home churches of the Southern District gathered good used clothing and made quilts and comforters and sent them to the Valley. Once a month or so the missionaries gathered to sort the clothing for the churches. The missionaries took the clothes home so people could choose what they needed. Whenever Anglo folks would move away from Premont, they brought many things they could not take such as dishes, pots and pans. These were eagerly picked up by people who regularly visited the store.

In the Esau home in Premont a bedroom just off the garage was turned into a store. People were asked to pay a little, so they felt they had found a bargain.

The money that was collected through the store helped to take people to special hospitals or pay for medicines. One year so much clothing was on hand the Esaus had a garage sale and collected enough to pay for the Christmas treats which were given to everyone who came.

Many people also came for treatments for sprained ankles, wrists, fingers, sore arms or backs. Many were not Christians, so Anna Esau decided, "If you come to take my time and strength, I shall just keep on telling you about the Lord. If you don't like that, you will stay away." She had attentive patients; they got free medical services just for listening.

Henry also helped neighbors who needed to have something fixed. A few times he wired their homes so they had electric lights.

F. WORK AMONG THE SICK

During the fifties many people were without cars, and came to the Esaus to be taken to different towns. The Esaus charged nothing to take people to the doctor or to a hospital. They also visited people with tuberculosis in their homes and in the tuberculosis hospital, then located at Moore Air Base, north of Mission, Texas, in the Valley. The patients gladly listened to God's Word and were very glad to have them pray for them.

The Esaus had open doors to pray whenever someone was sick. The people reasoned, "If it does not help, it has cost us nothing." A case of prolonged illness of a family member was a good time to sow the Word. When an old man named Cleotilde who came to church had a stroke, Henry went to his house day after day and always found it filled with people. He greeted them, read Bible verses, prayed, said,

"God bless you," and left. One day, when Cleotilde was conscious, Henry and he held hands and Henry recited John 3:16 again and again. The sick man said, clearly enough to be understood, "Shall not perish, shall not perish," with a smile on his face.

Another example of this occurred when Paula Ruiz, a neighbor who wanted to be baptized, became sick and had an operation. The day before she was to come home from the hospital, she suffered a stroke. When she came home the doctor gave medicine which the Esaus kept in their refrigerator. Any time, day or night, someone might come to ask for help for Paula; they quickly boiled the syringe and went to give the shot. They did this for several years before she died of another stroke.

G. EVANGELISM AND OUTREACH

Shortly after the Esaus took over the work at Premont, Walter Gomez came to conduct a series of meetings in the little chapel. These were ended by a picnic, and a large number of parents came to hear the message. Inocencio Garcia came for pre-Easter services in April, 1950, which were well attended. Others who served as evangelists through the years were Harry Neufeld and Ricardo Zapata, who came as a team. Many homes were visited and one afternoon two grandmothers and one young mother accepted the Lord. One of these joined the Baptist mission near her home, and the other two moved away and joined other churches.

One summer an ex-priest from Nicaragua named Victor Ovando, who had joined the Mennonite (Old) Mission, came to conduct services. People came to hear an ex-priest, though some doubted he was telling the truth, so one night he told his conversion story. Sitting at their homes, people could hear for blocks around by means of a loud speaker.

Anna Esau often was invited to Stanley parties. At one they played a game called, "Do what you are requested." She was asked to pray. She answered, "Not for fun." "No," they answered. She did, and wove in the gospel. Later she received the prize for the best performance. Many of those present heard an evangelical prayer for the first time.

H. THE CONVERSION OF "BLACKY THE DRUNK"

Since Rafael Perez was darker than his family members, he was called "Blacky." The first time he heard about the gospel was when his little four-year-old son died, and the Esaus went to comfort the family.

The sorrow that came to him only drove him to drink more and more. When he contracted hepatitis, and was very sick, he had time to think and to read the Bible. Weary of his habit, and suffering from a liver ailment, he began to pray. He found peace and joy and left alcohol. He began to witness to his family. After he was well, he informed the Esaus he was coming to church to tell his conversion story. He had invited his relatives and friends to come hear it. They came and Rafael, unafraid, gave his testimony. Since all knew he no longer drank, they had to believe his story. A few weeks later, Emma, his wife, also accepted the Lord one evening in the chapel. Without fear, they dedicated their next child to the Lord. Rafael also witnessed to his mother, who was ill, and led her to the Lord. When she died the Esaus were called to conduct a short service the night before the funeral. The body was in the same house where his little son had lain. Many people awaited the women who were coming to say the rosary. Rafael and Henry Esau sat near the coffin while Anna went into the next room, which had a number of women sitting in it. She found a place where she could see into the lighted room.

After the women with the rosary left, Rafael stood unashamed beside his pastor and witnessed for his Lord. Henry next read from the Word and prayed and all paid attention. People continue to call Rafael "Blacky," but never again "the drunk."

I. THE MENNONITE BRETHREN MISSIONARIES AT PREMONT

Ricardo Peña was the first Mennonite Brethren missionary to come serve weekends at Premont during 1947-48. He brought the canosa (panel truck) to gather the people. He served for a little over a year.

Henry T. Esau was a native of Inman, Kansas and a member of the Mennonite Brethren Church of Buhler, Kansas. He met Anna Wilma Hiebert in 1931 at Fort Hays State University, where both were college seniors. They were married on August 13, 1933, at Ingalls, Kansas. During the depression years they farmed and worked in Buhler, Kansas, until 1944. During the war they both taught in western Kansas. In 1948 they and Kenneth arrived at Premont, Texas, on June 10 to begin mission work in the little chapel with the people that attended services held by Ricardo Peña.

The Esaus served in the mission they built until August, 1960. These twelve eventful years were filled with joys and disappointments. When support of the mission was shifted from the Southern District to the Mennonite Brethren Foreign Mission Board, the Premont Mission was not ready to be independent, and would have to be sold. The chapel and their home were sold to the Mennonite (Old) Mission.

The Lord opened a door to teach in Edinburg, Texas, and they moved into the second house at the Lull Mission Station, two miles north of the city. The Lull Station was an independent work which did not belong to the Southern District Conference. The Esaus had to wait until the Richard Fandrichs came to take their place in their beloved home and mission. Paul Wolgemuth moved them to Lull on August 19, 1960. The Alvin Neufelds had gone on vacation so they plunged right in and did what they could in a strange place with people they did not know. The Lord led them to serve in the Valley and help in the development of the Latin American Mennonite Brethren Conference. In 1962 they moved their second house from Premont to Edinburg just across from the school where Henry taught. The house was completely rebuilt and became their home until the Lord called Henry home on January 31, 1980. He was the first missionary to die in the Valley.

CHAPTER 8

THE CHURCH AT LA JOYA

A. EARLY EFFORTS THAT LED TO A WORK IN LA JOYA

For a number of years, youth from Los Ebanos had gone to the village of Havana, a mile west of the present town of La Joya. During 1948 Ricardo Peña and Ricardo Zapata held the first Bible school in Havana. There were a few believers in the village who went to the mission at Los Ebanos, but they longed for a church in their own village. An old abandoned school house was secured for them, and the following people from Los Ebanos taught: Ricardo Peña, Ricardo Zapata, Librada Mireles, Irene Mireles, Dalia Garza and Alvina Fast. After 1948, Ricardo Peña taught Sunday school and held mid-week services in the old school building, assisted by Harold and Rosina Warkentin. People were saved and some were baptized and became members of the Los Ebanos Church.

Because of the success of the work at Havana, the Mission Council, together with the Home Missions Committee, began to pray and seek ways and means to establish a church in this location. Since Havana was a small village, they looked at a new town named La Joya, which means "The Jewel."

B. THE TOWN OF LA JOYA

Named after a body of water called La Joya, the town of La Joya lies on Highway 83, west of Mission. In 1947 there was only one school building and a residence for the principal.

C. THE LA JOYA MENNONITE BRETHREN CHURCH

God worked in wondrous ways to answer the prayers of those asking for another church. In 1953 He moved the heart of a brother in Oklahoma to give an anonymous gift of money to build the church in La Joya.

Ricardo Peña bought two lots in La Joya on the corner of First Street and Garza Avenue for the church, just one block south of Highway 83 and across from the La Joya school. He also bought another lot for his own house. One Sunday afternoon in February, 1953, Ricardo and a group of local people, together with A.W. Epp, gathered at the site and held a ground-breaking service.

People from various northern churches, with some of the El Faro teachers, built the cement block walls and roof. The local people of the congregation were grateful to God for the many who came to help.

On June 26, 1953, Miss Carmen Villarreal joined Ricardo Peña in matrimony and also in the work at La Joya Church. They moved into a small house of their own next to the church.

March 7, 1954, was a great day for La Joya as well as for the other missions. The La Joya Church, though not completed, was dedicated. On that day Ricardo Peña said, "We are today not only dedicating another church building to the Lord, but we are the first and only church in the new lake view town of La Joya, Texas. We are happy to be first in this locality to bring the gospel of salvation. May this church ever remain a true lighthouse of God, pointing the way for many sinners." The church was large enough to have room for Sunday school classes to meet by themselves. The day the building was dedicated, Ricardo and Carmen Peña were ordained as native missionaries of the Mennonite Brethren field in the Valley of South Texas.

This first building served until 1968, when the La Joya, Chihuahua and Los Ebanos congregations merged to form a new La Joya Church. The old buildings in the villages of Chihuahua and Los Ebanos were dismantled and the material was used to build a new, larger church, designed by Alvin Neufeld, the following year. Since the La Joya Church was made of cement blocks, it could not be used in the new structure, and was taken down after the new one was ready.

The new church was dedicated on October 25, 1970, long before the interior was finished. Alfredo Tagle, and whoever else could help, finished the interior. The young people of the church paid for and put in an air conditioner. Dark pews, enough to fill the sizeable church, were installed after the group was able to afford them. A carpet was later installed over the cement floor. In the front, over the baptistry, are the words, "Alabad al Señor en su santuario," or "Praise the Lord in His Sanctuary." Finally, after years of work, saving and giving, the largest church of the conference was completed; the congregation paid off the loan in 1984.

The adjoining lots, which once belonged to Ricardo Peña and Yolanda Villarreal, were purchased and made into a parking lot for the congregation.

D. THE MERGING OF THREE CHURCHES TO FORM THE PRESENT LA JOYA CONGREGATION

The Los Ebanos church, pastored by Alfredo Tagle, was getting old by 1968; it either had to be repaired or a new building needed to be put up. The congregation voted for neither option, deciding instead to merge in 1968. The Chihuahua church was in better shape but, since Daniel Wirsche had left for Uruguay, there was no pastor. The church, led by Antonio Garcia, a deacon, and Wesley Wirsche, also decided to merge and began to meet at La Joya.

On May 12, 1968, La Joya invited the congregations of Los Ebanos and Chihuahua to celebrate Mother's Day together. At first each congregation worshipped in its own church on Sunday mornings and went to La Joya at night. It was not easy to leave their beloved churches! By July, 1968, both Los Ebanos and Chihuahua decided to try and see if they could meet on Sunday mornings; on November 8, 1968, the three churches merged and have worshipped together since then.

Yolanda Villarreal recalls it was an impressive sight when the Los Ebanos group from the west and Chihuahua from the east, joined La Joya to form a new and larger congregation.

E. WORK AMONG THE CHILDREN AND YOUTH AT LA JOYA CHURCH

Since La Joya was a new mission, it took time to get people to attend services. Carmen Peña began classes with the girls, giving them Bible instruction and teaching them various crafts. While she was in church, Ricardo stayed home with their small children; on nights when Ricardo had a class with the boys she kept the children at home. They also held Bible school during summer time, with help from El Faro teachers.

Ricardo gathered the teenagers for weekly meetings and, once a month, they went to El Faro for a Youth for Christ meeting, where all the youth of the Mennonite Brethren Churches met. This continued until El Faro closed in 1969. After that the youth met in one of the churches once a month and for conferences.

After the Peña family moved to take charge of the church in Mission begun by Inocencio Garcia, others served at La Joya.

When the La Joya Church received the members from Los Ebanos and Chihuahua to form a new larger congregation, the children's and youth work increased. Pastor Alfredo Tagle delegated youth activities to Wesley and Zita Wirsche, a work they did for years, except for a time the Domingo Villarreals took charge. A recent highlight occurred in 1983 when a large group went to the Estes Youth Retreat in Estes Park, Colorado.

The church also had classes for the older children and, for some time, Maria Luisa Peña taught them to paint plaques with Bible verses on them.

F. WORK AMONG WOMEN

Carmen Peña conducted the first meetings among women at La Joya. She taught them how to embroider and also gave them Bible instructions. These women continued their meetings after the Peñas left.

After the merger of the three churches, the women's work was greatly increased. Chihuahua had a large group of women, and Los Ebanos also had a good-sized group. Under the guidance of Ofelia Tagle, they formed a source of strength for the church. They had Bible study and prayer meetings and also learned to make various kinds of crafts which were sold to get money for various projects. In 1984, under the leadership of Zita Wirsche, the women began to study "Escudrinad Las Escrituras," course No. 102, "Guia y Glosario Para El Que Quiere Ganar Almas Para el Señor." Since the formation of a conference-wide women's organization in 1961, they meet with others twice a year, in spring and in fall. They often met at El Faro School until it closed; since then they meet in one of the churches.

G. EVANGELISTIC WORK AT LA JOYA

From its beginning, La Joya was interested in reaching out. Among those who came for extended revival services were Enrique Galvan, Carlos Calero, and the former missionary Henry F. Thomas, who returned to minister. They also had a good turn-out for singing groups, such as the Singing Terrys and a program by Tabor College Choir. Paulino Bernal, a native of Texas, used to have a dance band before he was saved; after his conversion he went to churches to give his testimony and many came to hear him. When he had services at La Joya, the church was full, with over five hundred packed into the sanctuary and overflow room.

H. THE WORKERS AT LA JOYA CHURCH

Ricardo Peña began the work at La Joya in 1953, working together with Carmen Villarreal after their marriage in 1953. They worked in La Joya until 1961, when they moved to Mission. Ricardo attended Tabor College for two years, taking Bible and commercial subjects. Carmen studied for a term at the Rio Grande Bible Institute.

The local mission board asked the Peñas (and their two sons) to move to Abram and take charge of the Chihuahua work while the Henry Thomas' went on furlough. They left in fall, 1956, and returned the summer of 1957, during which time a daughter was added to the family. Before the Thomas' returned, the Peñas moved back to La Joya. During their year of absence, Alfredo Tagle, as a single man, filled in for them. Three more children were later added to the Peña family (the children are Carlos, Freddy, Dina, Ricky, Becky and David). In 1961 they went to the Mission Church while the Inocencio Garcias moved to Garciasville. The Peñas lived in rented quarters until a parsonage was purchased on 1821 Thornton Avenue in Mission.

In September, 1958, Alfredo and Ofelia Guillen Tagle were married at Gomez Palacios, Durango, Mexico. As newlyweds, they moved into the little house belonging to Ricardo Peña, while the Peña family was on furlough. The Tagles stayed until July 31, 1959. The Peñas returned to La Joya and stayed until they went to Mission in 1961. After they left, the Administrative Board asked the John Ables from the Rio Grande Bible Institute to serve at La Joya on weekends.

Daniel and Geneva Kime moved to La Joya before El Faro School started in 1963. They served the church while Geneva taught in El Faro. He took care of their three young children, Kennert, Danny and

Alane. For about a year the Kimes had assisted in the Lull Church near Edinburg. They left in 1965 to go to the New Tribes Mission in Panama.

The Administrative Board asked Anselmo Salinas' family to move to La Joya after the Kimes left. Anselmo and Lucia Garcia Salinas served from 1964-67. He is a native of Mission and she of the village of Chihuahua.

When Yolanda Villarreal and Annie Dyck were no longer needed in McAllen they were asked to move to La Joya, settling into Yolanda's house. For two-and-a-half-years, from January, 1967 to May, 1969, Yolanda and Annie worked in the church and taught in El Faro as they were needed. Students from RGBI in Edinburg came to preach. When none came, Annie Dyck held a Bible study with the congregation until the merger. In August, 1968, the congregation voted to have Alfredo Tagle serve as pastor. Alfredo and Ofelia supported themselves for the larger part during this time. After fourteen-and-a-half years, Alfredo resigned in spring, 1983. The Tagles went north to follow a migrant teaching program of which Ofelia is a part. They returned to teach again in the Valley while Alfredo does cabinet work.

Shortly after the Tagles left, Inocencio and Adelia Oralia Garcia served at La Joya, the largest church of the conference. The church asked Garcia to continue and, on July 7, 1983, he was installed as pastor. The Garcias served for a year but were advised by a doctor to lay down the work, due to strain on his heart. He served until the end of April, 1984.

Wesley Wirsche served after the Garcias left. The church waited for Daniel and Elsie Wirsche to return from Uruguay and installed them on January 20, 1985.

CHAPTER 9

THE LULL (EDINBURG) MENNONITE BRETHREN CHURCH

A. THE VILLAGE OF LULL, A SUBURB OF EDINBURG

The village of Lull is around two miles north of Edinburg and a half mile west of Highway 281. This little town lies just west of a large ice plant, which used to be especially important for the fruit and vegetable growers. The plant employs some of the people who live in Lull.

When the Neufelds moved to Lull they were the only Anglos there and many of the houses were small, built of wood. There also were a few stores but no cantinas (saloons), although a man who owned several in Edinburg lived there. The village had only one church at first, a Baptist chapel, although a small Catholic Church was later added.

B. EARLY GOSPEL EFFORTS IN LULL

M.C. Ehlert, an independent Baptist Evangelist with a burden for the Latin Americans, went from place to place preaching from a tent. When he came to Lull and held revival meetings, people responded and a church was started. At one time they had ninety members, including many Mexicans who crossed the border without passports. After they later returned to Mexico, the building and the few remaining members were left by Rev. Ehlert to a Mexican pastor. When he left the church was closed. When Alvin and Ruth Neufeld came to the Rio Grande Bible Institute as students, Ehlert encouraged them to go to Lull, where they reopened the little chapel. A few former members returned and others began to attend. But the pastor who had been placed in charge of the chapel reappeared and the Neufelds had to find their own meeting place. When he again left, the church became the playhouse for the children and the young people of Lull; every window and bench was broken as well as a piano was played into pieces. It stood until hurricane Beulah tumbled it all down. The place was cleared and is still used at times for tent services.

C. THE MENNONITE BRETHREN MISSION STATION IN LULL

In 1951 Alvin and Ruth Neufeld and their son Philip and daughter Phoebe moved their trailer home beside the old Baptist Chapel in Lull. They served while he continued his Bible training in Rio Grande Bible Institute.

69

Alvin bought three lots for a house just north of Monte Cristo Road. When the house was built in 1952 it was connected to a tent in which they conducted services. As soon as possible they used only the house. Those first years while Alvin was learning Spanish, he preached in English and a young man, Alfredo Tagle, translated into Spanish.

People were saved and Alvin built an outdoor tank to serve as a baptistry. This later became a water reservoir, catching every dribble of water during the night from the Lull water system.

A church was built in 1953, on the northwest corner of Rodriguez and Fuentes, with money from special gifts outside of the budget of Southern District Mission Board. Since the lots also were paid for by other means, the Lull Mission was not a part of the same organization as the missions at Los Ebanos, Chihuahua, La Grulla, and Premont. Alvin Neufeld incorporated this church.

During Hurricane Beulah in 1967, the church was damaged and the tower was removed. Mennonite Disaster Service workers from the north came and put on a new roof.

During the time Anselmo Salinas served Lull, the frame church was reinforced. The entire building was bricked from the outside, new windows were put in and the inside was redecorated.

In 1982 Redge Willems did a great deal of work on the parsonage, which had been neglected. They extended the roof over one part that had a flat roof and stopped the leaking.

Soon after the organization of the Latin Conference, Alvin began steps to transfer the Lull church and the parsonage to LAMB. Negotiations were begun in 1964 and were completed as soon as the church had paid off the loan for the Sunday school addition.

Alvin Neufeld later built another house just east of the church, facing Fuentes street. Built by Paul Jury, a language student at RGBI, and Alvin during March and May, 1958, it became home for the Paul Jury family. The H.T. Esaus and Daniel Kimes also lived in this house before it was moved to Pharr.

D. THE WORK AMONG CHILDREN AT LULL

Sunday school classes were started as soon as possible and soon regular services were conducted in Spanish. Alvin and Paul Jury began Christian Service brigade Clubs with boys, while Ruth Neufeld began Pioneer Girls Clubs. There also were regular Bible classes on Wednesday nights with classes for each age group. In 1960, when all missionaries were withdrawn from the field, the Neufeld's mission was exempt and the Esaus found a place of service in Lull. Since both the Neufelds and the Esaus were self-supporting, the work could continue. Alvin worked at various trades until he bought a water softener business servicing homes; Henry taught in Lamar School in Edinburg for eleven years, until he retired in 1971.

The church added a Sunday school wing in 1961 to better meet demands for the various classes. The Esaus and Neufelds served together. One couple took care of the preaching and the other looked after the educational work in the church. After two years the Esaus built a home in Edinburg, just across the street from Lamar School, and they continued their work in Lull.

Each year Anna Esau designed a new set of masters of plaques to suit each grade and to correlate with the theme of the Bible school. Many children from homes where parents would not come to church allowed the children to come to Bible school because they could paint. The plaques were always retouched and varnished so they were beautiful. The parents were proud of what their children had done and put them up in their homes, giving them Bible verses to look at.

Since summer time was free, the Esaus could devote it to the church, while Alvin Neufeld had to work. They went to help other churches and conducted two or three Bible schools a season. Both taught Bible, nature study or craft at Camp Loma de Vida for a number of years.

The Alvin Neufelds moved to McAllen in October, 1963, to begin a new work. Inocencio and Amelia Garcia and daughters Maria, Lydia and Elisa came to Lull every Sunday from their home in Chihuahua. They moved into the parsonage in January, 1964.

The work continued much as before. Inocencio Garcia did the preaching and visiting work while the Esaus took care of the Sunday Services / Wednesday night classes and clubs for the youth and children.

Juanita Cortez Garcia, a daughter-in-law of Inocencio Garcia, was a great help in the church. She always taught a class and often told stories to the children on Sunday night and helped young people with dramas.

Inocencio Garcia was concerned that Garciasville was without a pastor so, in September, 1972, the Esaus accepted a call from La Iglesia de Gracia in Garciasville and left the work at Lull to the Inocencio Garcia family. The Esaus came back every year to conduct Vacation Bible school at Lull, even after the Inocencio Garcia family left and Anselmo and Lucia Salinas had taken over the work.

Inocencio and Amelia Garcia left Lull because of her ill health and moved to Chihuahua, their old home village. They built a house on the very church floor that had been left when the Chihuahua congregation merged with La Joya in 1968. Amelia died unexpectedly on August 5, 1974. Anselmo and Lucia Garcia Salinas took over the work at Lull and carried on until 1979. They did much to improve the church building, had extra Bible schools and evangelistic meetings.

After Crispin Diaz served the church, a group of Christian students from Pan American University came to teach the children on Friday nights. They taught Bible and crafts. The young people attend the monthly CYF (Christian Youth Fellowship) at the various churches.

E. WORK AMONG WOMEN IN THE LULL CHURCH

During the time that the Neufelds and Esaus served together, there were Bible classes for the women of the church and those they brought along. Ruth Neufeld and Anna Esau stressed Bible memory work and, with the group, studied Bible portions. Anna Esau made charts to help the women understand. After the Inocencio Garcias came, the women did handwork of various kinds. In 1983 Angela Diaz began Bible studies with the women of the village.

F. EVANGELISM IN LULL MENNONITE BRETHREN CHURCH

From the beginning, evangelism was of utmost importance. People came to the meetings, even though some just out of curiosity or, sometimes, even to hinder others. Some chose to receive the Lord.

Among the early converts was Alfredo Tagle, who became one of the leaders of the Conference. Among evangelists who returned were Zerral Brown, Enrique Galvan, Jesse Guerra, a native of the work at Garciasville, Wilfred Thiessen, and others.

For three years during the latter 50s and early 60s an opportunity for witness arose just across from the Lull Church on Monte Cristo Road. Some two thousand men from Mexico who worked at different ranches during the day, were housed there in a camp. Alvin began to preach to them and had their attention until some one stirred them up against him by calling him names. One time he was even stoned, and his car windshield was broken. As a result he spoke to them by means of a loud speaker. Many of them came to church on Sunday nights and around five hundred signed decision cards. Even after all had returned to Mexico, Alvin remained in contact with several for some time.

RGBI students also assisted the pastor by visiting each home in the village with him to present tracts. In this way new ones who entered the village became acquainted with the gospel and were invited to attend services. Through the years each pastor and his wife visited as they were able. In 1981 the church used three gospel movies in place of preaching.

G. WORK AMONG THE SICK IN LULL

Ruth Neufeld took sick people to the doctor. One time she was called to a very emotionally upset member. She came and called Anna Esau to help, so both worked with the sister. She was very cold so they used her electric blanket and also massaged her limbs, praying with her, claiming God's power to heal. The patient fell asleep and that spell was over.

Alvin and Ruth also spent much time with Mrs. Palacios, who was blind, teaching her to read braille. She did learn and, one time, read a portion in church.

H. THE PASTORS AND WORKERS OF THE LULL MENNONITE BRETHREN CHURCH

Alvin and Ruth Heidebrecht Neufeld belonged to the Ingalls (later at Cimarron) Kansas, Mennonite Brethren Church. Alvin went to Tabor College for one year, in 1949, where they met Walter Gomez, then at the Rio Grande Bible Institute, who encouraged them to come to school in the Valley. They arrived on October 23, 1950, with two small children, Philip and Phoebe. M.C. Ehlert later directed them to Lull. In 1953 they were ordained as missionaries at Ingalls, Kansas, in their home church.

Alvin built another house on the station when the Paul Jury family came to assist. They stayed two years (1958-1960). Henry T. and Anna Esau lived in that house for two years before moving to Edinburg in 1962. That year Daniel and Geneva Kime and three children moved into the second house at Lull to assist where needed. They stayed a year, then left for the La Joya Church.

The Neufelds served twelve years, from 1951-63, until they moved to McAllen with five children, Philip, Phoebe, Naomi Jean, Becky and Paul Stanley. In 1960, when all Anglo missionaries were removed from the Texas field, the Esaus found a work at the Lull station, which was not Conference property. They served in Lull from 1960-72, at which time they accepted a call from Iglesia de Gracia, in Garciasville, in the upper Valley near Rio Grande City.

After the Neufelds left in October, 1963, Inocencio and Amelia Garcia and three daughters, Maria, Lydia, and Elisa moved to Lull in January, 1964. They came from the Chihuahua Church where they had been taught by Henry and Ruth Thomas. The Garcias had also opened the work in Mission and served there from 1953-61.

The Garcias came to Lull soon after the Neufelds left in October, 1963, but did not move until January, 1964. They stayed there for eleven years, until Amelia was too ill to help carry on. They moved back to their old village at Chihuahua. She died unexpectedly on August 5, 1974, while Inocencio Garcia was filling in at Garciasville during a brief vacation of the Esaus.

The next pastors at Lull were Anselmo (a native of Mission) and Lucia Salinas, a daughter of Inocencio Garcia. Anselmo was ordained at Lull on May 18, 1975 and they served from 1974-79.

Israel Montemajor came in September, 1979. He stayed until Easter, 1980.

When there was no pastor, Ramon Flores served or found someone else to serve.

Redge and Ive Willems began to work in September, 1979, while students at RGBI. Although from Canada, they had been working in Mexico and, therefore, knew the Spanish. Redge was also still studying in Rio Grande Bible Institute. They did what they could to regather the scattered flock before leaving to join Wycliffe translators.

Crispin Diaz had served at the Mennonite Brethren Church in

Mission for several years. They left and moved to Edinburg and attended Lull Church, helping where possible. When the Willems decided to leave, the church called Crispin and Angela Diaz, installing them on October 24, 1982. They did good work.

I. A CONVERSION STORY IN THE LULL CHURCH

Ramon Flores was one of the boys who attended the Christian Service Brigade Clubs in Lull. Ramon made a profession of faith and meant it at that time. But, while in high school, he quit church and ran with the crowd. At first it was only little things he knew were wrong but, as time went on, his lifestyle became worse and worse. He worked as a meat cutter in one of the Edinburg stores and married, but kept up his night life. The Lord, however, followed his erring sheep, sending people his way to witness to him and do all they could to restore him to the Lord.

Parties seemed to rule his life — even when his children were sick, he had to go to a party. His drinking began to cause him to have blackouts. He would awaken in the morning and find himself lying with his shoes on, and he did not know how he had gotten home. The spells continued until he became afraid he would be killed or he would kill someone else. His fear was very real. Then, at last, he said "Yes" to the Lord. "Take me, I am yours." He was delivered from his evil habits and the blackouts.

One Sunday, when Inocencio Garcia was pastor, he brought his family to the Lull church, eager to learn more about God's Word. Ramon has had many trials, but he has remained faithful to the Lord, useful in the church and serves on various Conference boards.

CHAPTER TEN

THE MENNONITE BRETHREN CHURCH AT CASITA AND GARCIASVILLE

A. THE VILLAGES OF GARCIASVILLE AND CASITA

The villages of Garciasville and Casita (little house) are old and join each other. A paved road going to Rio Grande City makes a loop off Highway 83 entering Garciasville at the east end and runs through Casita, which forms the western part of the twin villages.

The villages have their own cemeteries and used to have their own churches. When a big new church was built it was placed near Garciasville just inside Casita. An elementary school named La Union was located partly in each village, establishing a union between the people of the two communities. Garciasville is the smaller of the two, but it has a government post office. The people living in Garciasville get their mail from the post office while those in Casita have rural delivery from Rio Grande City.

As a whole, the homes are well built and kept in good order. The La Casita Farms, a huge corporation renting small acreages of land belonging to various people, gives work to many living in the villages.

During cantaloupe harvest many of the village girls and women work in the packing sheds, while others are out in the fields.

There are a good number of the church men and women who work in the various schools in Rio Grande City and the various villages of Starr County.

B. EARLY EFFORTS TO PROCLAIM THE GOSPEL IN GARCIASVILLE AND CASITA

The inhabitants of the twin villages had the opportunity to hear the gospel years before the arrival of the first Mennonite Brethren missionaries. Harry Neufeld found one member, Lindita, a Methodist, who could sing song after song and recite long portions of the Bible.

Neufeld came to the Rio Grande Valley in 1937, looking for a location to open a mission. In Rio Grande City he met V.Y. Dickenson, a Methodist missionary. From him he learned that no group had established an evangelistic congregation in any of the villages lying along the Rio Grande from Mission to Rio Grande City. In the cities, however, several denominations had succeeded in planting churches among the Spanish-speaking people.

Shortly after coming to the Valley, Neufeld took Inocencio Garcia to visit many villages to learn of their spiritual needs. In La Grulla and Garciasville they found unused Methodist chapels. Permission was later obtained for some of the Los Ebanos youth to conduct Sunday school in the afternoons as well as Bible school in one chapel, which stood only a short distance to the east of the present La Iglesia de Gracia Mennonite Brethren Church.

Ricardo Peña and others soon had a nice group attending. The Ruben Wedels helped to conduct Vacation Bible school, which also was well attended. When the Methodists again sent their own workers to Garciasville, the Mennonite Brethren withdrew. The chapel was later closed but, from the place, which now is only brush, the gospel was preached in Garciasville. Several of those who attended Sunday school and Bible school at that place have become members of the Mennonite Brethren Church.

In Casita another gospel work had been begun and Brother Vera had built a small block church, which still stands. This group had also lost its workers. One day Brother Vera called at the Peña store in Los Ebanos and asked for help. Soon after that invitation, Harold Warkentin and Ricardo Peña conducted services in Casita.

C. THE MISSION STATION THAT BECAME KNOWN AS THE CASITA MENNONITE BRETHREN CHURCH AND LATER "LA IGLESIA DE GRACIA"

After Brother Vera came to Los Ebanos and asked for help, and offered the use of his little church, the local missionary board decided that they needed some form of security before they began another work. So they leased the ground and the small building for ten years.

In 1949 Ricardo Peña and Harold Warkentin went to Casita to conduct services. Ricardo stayed to help preach in Spanish after the Albert Epps had been asked by the local board to also go to Casita.

The Epps lived on the El Faro grounds and went to Casita for the various meetings to help teach together with others who knew Spanish.

The first time the Epps went, they took the Ruben Wedels along and gathered up some people. That group continued to come and formed the Mennonite Brethren Church of Casita. Ricardo Peña helped the Epps preach in Spanish while Otila and Maria Elena Villarreal helped teach, sing and play the piano.

In 1952 Ricardo and Grace Zapata came from Los Ebanos, where they had served a year during the furlough of Harry and Sarah Neufeld. They lived in a rented house in Casita and visited people.

Ricardo Zapata reported in 1953, in the El Faro newsletter, that believers at Santa Cruz and ranches nearby were interested in worshiping with the Casita group. Since it was easier to take them to the church than begin a new group, they brought them in a bus. Ricardo Zapata also held meetings west of Rio Grande City, known as Garcias de Arriba.

In 1954 the Zapatas left the work and moved to Edinburg, Texas,

to begin an educational career, but the Epps continued to attend at
Casita. Since the little church had become too small, a group of men
from Oklahoma came and put down a cement floor and built a wooden
tabernacle over it. This chapel, dedicated November 29, 1953, gave
room for everyone who came to services. Sunday school rooms were
also built inside the little Vera church.

John and Daphyn (Dafina) Savoia came to pastor the Casita
church in 1954 and left after sixteen months to go to La Grulla. They
also lived in a rented house in Casita.

After the Savoias left in 1956, the Epps took over the work. In
1957 they moved a small house from El Faro to a plot of ground on
the north side of the road that runs through the villages. The move
allowed them to be near the church and have more contact with the
people of the villages of Casita and Garciasville. Albert continued to
teach at El Faro.

Before the ten years were up, the chapel on the Vera lot was
moved on to a new cement floor in Garciasville. The congregation
finished the inside and put tiles on the floor and, as soon as they could,
added Sunday school rooms to the back.

Albert Epp worked after school and weekends on the ground and
provided a ball diamond and other places for games for the youth of
the twin villages.

After Anselmo Salinas left Garciasville, the church had only
weekend pastors for some years and the buildings were not well maintained. The church was in need of repairs when Pedro Durik was in
charge, and he and others began to plan a new church. But the congregation deciding against going into debt, worked and gave to buy materials for renovations. Albert Epp of Corn, Oklahoma, came with others
to spend their winter vacation working on the Garciasville church,
which had been renamed, "La Iglesia de Gracia," during Pedro Durik's
stay. Early in 1972 they put on a new roof and extended the walls of
the Sunday School rooms to include a kitchen and indoor rest rooms.
Later the people of the church put in a ceiling in the sanctuary, but
much was still left to be done. When the H.T. Esaus came in September, 1972, they patched up holes so they could keep warm during
cold spells. Two church members helped to lay the fuel line to the
heater.

The Epps came with a group year after year. In 1976 they came
in February to add an extension to the south end of the church, making
a foyer and an extra room for a nursery. The entrance was moved from
the south to the east side of the church. Henry and Anna Esau spent
time varnishing the woodwork which Inocencio Garcia had put into
the new part. The Ed Vogts from Corn, Oklahoma, supplied white
padded second-hand pews which beautified the interior of the
sanctuary. During the time the Esaus had their last Bible school, two
men came to brick the entire building, making a cross in the south
wall, to show that it is a church. All worked hard to be ready for
August 1, 1976, when the church was dedicated and the congregation

observed the twenty-fifth anniversary of the coming of the Epps to
Casita. The Epp family was all there for the celebration, enjoying an
unforgettable reunion.

Since then shrubs and flowers have been planted around the
church, while on the inside they put in a baptistry, stage, carpet, air-
conditioners and a loud speaker. Inocencio Garcia and the youth
cleared the brush off the large back yard and made it into a park with
a shelter house and barbecue pit; the park was dedicated the evening
Carlos Roman was installed in October, 1982. In 1984 the church built
a three-room addition to the north. The church later painted these
rooms and the back of the church which does not have bricks.

D. THE WORK DONE AMONG THE CHILDREN AT CASITA
AND GARCIASVILLE

From the beginning, Sunday school classes were started for each
age group, with teachers coming from Los Ebanos and El Faro school.
Music was very important and many hymns and choruses were taught.
In summer there were Vacation Bible schools with good attendance.

After the Epps moved to Garciasville, they had more time to devote to the children. On Friday nights they had classes for juniors,
including time playing games outside. One of those boys, Jesse Guerra,
later became an evangelist. Emily Epp also had a class for young girls,
teaching Bible and various kinds of crafts.

During 1973-76 there were large Bible schools. Children came to
listen to the mission story told by Anna Esau and to paint gospel
plaques. Many beautiful plaques went out into homes of those who
never came to any services.

During the time Inocencio and Oralia Garcia served at Iglesia de
Gracia, they had weekly Bible study and recreation with the youth,
together they had six Sunday school classes. They also encouraged the
children to attend Camp Loma de Vida, and a good number went.

E. WORK AMONG WOMEN

The work with women took various forms — Emily Epp did what
she could to help mothers, and the women at Casita and later at Garciasville were organized as a circle when Alfredo and Ofelia Tagle
served the church. Sometimes the older women as well as the young
ones and girls in the church as well as some men came together to
prepare a big tamale supper with all the rest of good Mexican foods.
They sold plates and about the entire village came to eat or buy plates
to take home. The proceeds went to the building fund.

F. WORK AMONG THE YOUTH

Through the years something was always done for the youth. They
attended Youth for Christ meetings held at El Faro for all the young
people from the churches, where they had a period of entertainment,

games and contests followed by some good messages for all. Youth from Garciasville also took part in these meetings.

One group at Garciasville raised money and put a new rug on the stage of the church. During the early 1980s, the youth worked and sold chicken bar-b-que to raise money to send six young people to Estes 83 in Estes Park, Colorado. Carlos Ramon, a full-time pastor since October, 1982, is continuing the Friday evening meetings with the young people.

G. EVANGELISM AND OUTREACH

From the beginning at Casita, there was some form of evangelism. Ricardo Zapata held well-attended open air services west of Rio Grande City in a town known as Garcias de Arriba. During the time John Savoia served at Casita, he went several miles west to a small chapel built just below a bluff. On its top the church had a tall cross that came to be known as "La Santa Cruz", or "Holy Cross." People climbed the steep hill to pay vows.

During the time Pedro Durik served he took students and young people out Sunday afternoons to various places to witness.

During the years of 1972-73, while the Esaus served the church, evangelistic services were emphasized, both in the church and out in the village plaza. Lights were strung around the outside of a stage and seating area and many people came to hear a choir and listen to a gospel message. The plaza was cleared each night after the service, with the piano remaining on a trailer so it could be taken into a garage of one of the members. The speaker, Jesús (Jesse) Guerra, a native of Garciasville, had a real burden for the people of his native villages. Many came forward to pray.

H. THE MISSIONARIES AND PASTORS OF THE MENNONITE BRETHREN WORK AT CASITA AND GARCIASVILLE

Ricardo Peña, a member of Los Ebanos church, the first native worker to be accepted by the Southern District Conference (in 1947), worked for several years where he was needed before he and Harold Warkentin began services at the little Vera church in Casita.

Ricardo Zapata also was of the early workers from Los Ebanos. He met Grace Hiebert at Tabor College and, after they married, went to live in Casita in 1952 after a year's service in Los Ebanos. They left mission work in 1954 and moved to Edinburg, Texas, to teach. During that time he acquired a Masters Degree from Kingsville. With two children, they moved to Reedley, California, to work in schools.

In 1954 John and Daphyn (Dafina) Smith Savoia came to take over the pastorate at Casita. Through Alvin Neufeld the Savoias were introduced to Casita. When La Grulla station needed a pastor in 1956, the Savoias were asked to take over the work begun by Ruben and Eva Wedel.

The opening of El Faro school in 1948 brought teachers who also were missionaries, such as Albert and Emily Bartel Epp, to Casita. After two years at Tabor College, the Epps, with their children, Gloria, Mary Lou, and Barbara, went to help build El Faro School in 1948. "The Lord really prepared us at that time to come back and work here," said Albert. They returned to Tabor for two more years, until Albert graduated, and on July 13, 1951, packed up and moved to El Faro School. They lived in the teacherage on the school grounds for six years and drove out to Casita for services. After they built a house at the new location in Garciasville, they moved there in 1957. In 1961 they moved to Corn, Oklahoma, but left their hearts behind. Albert taught in Corn Bible School for some years until he became pastor of the Corn Mennonite Brethren Church.

In July, 1961, the Garciasville Church called Inocencio Garcia. Inocencio and Amelia Garcia and family went to live in the parsonage for one year. They had lived in Chihuahua and had begun the work at Mission. They moved back to the village and supported themselves in Chihuahua until they moved to Lull.

Alfredo and Ofelia Guillen Tagle, who were stationed in La Grulla, came to take care of the congregation after Inocencio left the church. Alfredo, a native of Lull, and Ofelia, from Mexico, are both Rio Grande Bible Institute graduates. They continued in Garciasville until August 15, 1964, when they left to study in Torreon, Mexico.

David Fast moved into the parsonage in 1962, and soon after married Martha Kroeker, a Mennonite Brethren missionary from Colombia. They both taught in El Faro during those years (although Martha only taught part of the time). They left in June, 1966, with son Paul to take an assignment in Panama, where they still serve (1984).

For several months the church was without a pastor. By January, 1967, Anselmo and Lucia Garcia Salinas left their work at La Joya and moved into the parsonage at Garciasville. He was a member of the Mission Mennonite Brethren Church and she grew up in Chihuahua but attended the Mission congregation. They served a year-and-a-half, until July, 1968.

Some students from RGBI came to help keep the church open on Sundays. Simón Rada worked for some time until he was transferred to Donna in 1968. Pedro Durik served in November, 1968. He came every Sunday, bringing some students to assist him. The church was named "Iglesia de Gracia" (Grace Church), while Pedro Durik served. He also organized a church council which still serves. The Duriks moved to Leesburg, Indiana, where they prepare Christian literature for Spanish-speaking people.

Alfredo and Rosa Bahena preached for five months before it became necessary for him to return to Mexico.

Leonel Saenz was in charge of the church until September, 1972, when Henry and Anna Esau began to serve at La Iglesia de Gracia in Garciasville. They stayed in the parsonage on weekends and for whole weeks, when there were revival meetings, Bible schools, or work crews from Oklahoma. They came from the Lull church where they had served for twelve years. Illness forced them to retire to their home in Edinburg, Texas, in 1976.

Inocencio and Adela Oralia Garcia took charge of the church in May, 1976. They lived in their home in McAllen and drove to work at Garciasville. After a heart attack in 1982, he had to give up his active work.

Carlos and Emma de Leon Roman, with children Carlos Armando and Jessica, were installed on October 23, 1982. They were the first missionaries in Reynosa, Mexico, who began a work for the Latin American Mennonite Brethren in 1977. He had attended seminary in La Puente, California, and held several pastorates in Mexico.

CHAPTER 11

THE MENNONITE BRETHREN CHURCH AT MISSION

A. EARLY EVENTS THAT LED TO THE OPENING OF A WORK AT MISSION

The Chihuahua mission had members who lived on the west side of the city of Mission who had to be transported to church, which took time and money. So Henry Thomas and Inocencio Garcia began to think and pray about opening a work in the city of Mission for them and others.

Soon after the ordination of Inocencio and Amelia Garcia on December 28, 1952, they began to look for a place to locate a church in Mission. They bought several lots on Perez Street since there seemed to be good possibilities for growth in the Bonita Addition, to the west side of the city. However, a chemical plant bought a large tract to the north and so it was left bare.

B. THE CITY OF MISSION

The city began years ago when the Spanish built a mission to Christianize the inhabitants of the territory. Priests are said to have planted the first citrus trees in the Valley. In time the region about this old church became known as Mission.

The city of Mission lies just west of McAllen, although, traveling west on Highway 83, one does not notice leaving one city and entering the other. The same signpost that has McAllen on the east side, says Mission on the west.

Many Anglos live in Mission, as compared to Rio Grande City. Mission has its own hospital and schools for all its citizens. There are many trailer parks in and around Mission which teem with life in winter. Every type of recreation is provided. In some parks they have Bible classes for all who wish to attend.

C. THE MISSION MENNONITE BRETHREN CHURCH

Inocencio Garcia held his first service in Mission on December 11, 1953, in the back yard of Santos Ybarra's residence on Pueblo Street. The group met at this place until Henry Thomas and Inocencio Garcia bought a lot a block to the north on Perez Street. Aaron A. Dick, the father of Mrs. Henry Thomas, paid for the lot, but the congregation bought the lot next to it to provide more space for a church yard. The little church from Chihuahua was moved on to the lots and Harry

Neufeld let them use a small trailer house for Sunday school classes. These buildings soon became too small and, in the winter of 1957, Victor Fast from Adams, Oklahoma, came to begin a new, much larger church. He finished the building the next winter and the church was dedicated in 1959. No parsonage was built, since the Garcia family had their own home in Chihuahua. But when the Ricardo Peña family came to serve at Mission in 1961, there was no place for them to live. The Penas sold their small home, near the La Joya church, and used the money for a down payment on a house at 1812 Thornton Avenue in Mission. This home still is the parsonage for the pastor of the Mennonite Brethren Church in Mission.

The growth that was expected at the Bonita Addition never came, putting the church on the very edge of that section of Mission and Perez Street was left narrow and unimproved. The congregation continued to function until it could buy lots on Holland Avenue, just across from Pearson Elementary school. Ricardo Peña bought three lots for $1,800 and, since he was working for a gravel company at the time, was given material to make foundations and floors for the church at the new location. On April 17, 1972, the floors were poured for the rebuilt church. The sanctuary faces north as it had on Perez Street, and the front entrance is in the new addition. Double glass doors facing west make it inviting to enter. The entire building was covered with white bricks. The church has a sign that reads, "Iglesia Evangelica, Hermanos Mennonitas 300 Holland Ave." (Evangelical Church, Mennonite Brethren).

The inside was paneled around new windows and a carpeted stage crosses the front (except for an exit to the back east door), with enough space left for the piano. Later, window air conditioners were installed. The foyer is in the new addition, along with a kitchen with cabinets, Sunday School rooms, and restrooms to make it modern. Ricardo Peña got so much material free or at cost that the church was rebuilt for $8,000. Leander Bargen from Mountain Lake, Minnesota did a great deal of the work, with the Peña family and some other members helping when possible. Edd Vogt from Corn, Oklahoma, also built cabinets for the kitchen. He also filled the church with white padded pews.

D. THE WORK AMONG CHILDREN AND ADULTS IN THE MENNONITE BRETHREN CHURCH AT MISSION

The Inocencio Garcias started Sunday school classes as soon as they had enough pupils and teachers. A church was organized on May 15, 1955, with seven baptized members. After the new church was built, the old one provided room for classes for all ages. During summer time, there were Vacation Bible schools. These always attracted some children who had not been permitted to attend church services. Jonas Ybarra was the first Sunday school superintendent and Natividad Garcia led the singing. They also had a mid-week service for those who came. In 1961 the Peña family took over the work of the church and continued what had been started. As soon as their children were old enough, they helped in one way or another.

Ricardo Peña worked to support his family, but always found time to visit here and there coming or going to work.

When Crispin and Angela Diaz came in 1978, they had Sunday school and Bible clubs on Friday night for nine to thirteen-year olds in the parsonage.

John and Becky Wall came to the church at Mission in November, 1981, and they worked with children in special classes on Wednesday nights. They sing, have a Bible lesson and some craft.

E. WORK AMONG THE WOMEN

As soon as there were enough women, the Garcias had a service for them on Thursday nights. Amelia had projects, such as sewing, for part of the evening, then Inocencio would come and give a short devotional message. They closed with prayer.

After 1961, when the Peñas came, Carmen taught the ladies how to embroider and make beautiful aprons and other things. Some of these items were taken to the Women's Conference and sold. Carmen also helped the women to organize and they have continued through the years.

F. WORK AMONG THE YOUTH IN MISSION

The Garcias took their young people to the meeting on Saturday night at El Faro with youth from the other churches. Ricardo Peña also met with the youth Friday nights. Carmen helped them to put on Christian plays and dramas at Christmas, Easter, and other times. They used light and sound effects as well as stage settings and costumes. The group went to other places to perform.

G. EVANGELISM AT MISSION MENNONITE BRETHREN CHURCH

Since Mission was a new work, the Inocencio Garcias did a great deal of visiting to get to know people. They also had special meetings in the church. Among the evangelists were David Cooper and G. Bello from Nuevo Ideal, Mexico, one of the Foreign Mission Board stations. Other evangelists were Alfonzo Ruiz, of Mexico City, and Warren William Coles, a Bible teacher, who came year after year to conduct a series of meetings.

While the Crispin Diaz family was at Mission they also had evangelistic meetings and went to conduct meetings in Abram once a week. They visited in the hospital. The John Walls have had special meetings each year in the church.

H. THE MISSIONARIES, DEACONS AND WORKERS AT MISSION

Inocencio and Amelia Garcia were among the first members in the church in Chihuahua pastored by Henry and Ruth Thomas. After Inocencio served as assistant pastor in Chihuahua, they began work in the city of Mission in 1953 (when they had five children — Inocencio Jr., Natividad, Lucia, Maria, Lydia and Elisa). They did the pioneer work for the church at Mission and served until 1961.

In August, 1961, Ricardo and Carmen Villarreal Peña came from the La Joya church, which they had started. Ricardo, one of the early converts of Los Ebanos, and Carmen, of La Grulla, first lived in a housing project called Mission Acres, and also in Anagua Village, before the parsonage on 1812 Thornton Avenue was bought by the church. They served even when Carmen was very ill. Their six children, Carlos, Freddy, Dina, Ricky, Becky and David grew up in the Mission church.

During the years Ricardo Peña served the Mission church, they had two ordained deacons, Pedro Ibarra and Juan Cortez, who later moved to California. Ricardo Peña resigned from the church in 1977, leaving it well organized. Inez Ibarra, member of the church council and moderator of the church, was put in charge until a pastor could be found. Crispin Diaz of Lansing, Michigan, was recommended to Ricardo Peña, who invited Crispin and Angela Diaz to come in 1978, about a year after the Peñas had resigned. The Diaz's have two children, Daniel and Ruthy.

During the time the Diaz family served at Mission, six deacons and deaconesses were appointed — Federico and Aurelia Garcia, Inez Ibarra, Rodulfo Peña, Maria Alicia Alberas and Francica Cabrera.

The Diaz family resigned in 1981 and went to take charge of the Lull church.

John and Becky Neufeld Wall began their service at the Mission church on November 8, 1981. Johan (John) Wall is a native of the Nuevo Ideal, Durango, Mexico; Becky is the daughter of Alvin and Ruth Neufeld, the first missionaries of the Lull M.B. Church. They had the privilege of spending their honeymoon in service in Spain in the summer of 1981.

Arthur and Helen Dalke came to the Mission Church in 1978, after working in Cuba and with TEAM, The Evangelical Alliance Mission, in Venezuela, South America. They had a group in Mexico which now worships with the LAMB mission in Reynosa. They have a correspondence school in Mexico called "Light of Life" courses. He taught the adult class in the Mission church and directed the singing, while she played the piano. They left in February, 1984.

CHAPTER 12

THE PHARR MENNONITE BRETHREN CHURCH

A. EARLY EVENTS THAT LED TO THE FORMATION OF A MENNONITE BRETHREN CHURCH IN PHARR

McAllen, the largest city west of Highway 281, is the commercial and medical center of the Upper Valley with several banks and two large hospitals, as well as smaller ones and nursing homes. Medical specialists of every kind live and work in McAllen.

McAllen is on the American side of the international bridge over the Rio Grande at Hidalgo. Custom houses are located on each side. McAllen also has a large airport from which jet planes come and go to the Valley.

After Alvin and Ruth Neufeld had served twelve years in the village of Lull, they moved on to start another church. The family with five children moved to 1214 North Main in McAllen on October 11, 1963. Several workers gathered in that home to ask God's guidance for the beginning of a Mennonite Brethren congregation in McAllen, Texas.

By spring, 1964, a residence was rented at 1718 Maple Street. After some remodeling, weekly services were begun. The Conference supported Alvin Neufeld as pastor; Ruben and Eva Wedel served as assistant pastor and both taught to support themselves.

During the time the Neufelds worked in McAllen and had services on Maple Street, there were some who accepted the Lord and others who rejected the message. The services were held in the large room and Sunday school classes in the smaller ones. When the Southern District Area Conference subsidy was discontinued, the group met in the parsonage at 504 Baywood for over a year. People crowded in among the furniture in the pastor's home. The family of a widow, Altagracia Villarreal, with ten children, a number of them believers from the mission at San Miguel (now Diaz Ordaz) in Mexico, formed a nucleus for the congregation.

B. THE CITY OF PHARR

The city of Pharr is scattered over a large territory. It has stores, banks, and what is found in most places in the Valley. The High School is called P.S.J.A. for Pharr, San Juan, and Alamo. It is east of Pharr on Highway 83. The office of Children's Haven International is on South Cage, not far from the Suderman Clinic. There are churches of the major denominations, both Spanish and English.

Pharr, with some 20,000 people, lies mostly south of Expressway 83, and a very long overpass leaves Pharr and ends in McAllen.

C. THE ORGANIZATION OF THE PHARR MENNONITE BRETHREN CHURCH

When the Neufelds began to work in McAllen under the Mennonite Brethren Mission Board, he thought it best to sell his water softener business, but kept his building in Pharr on W 813 FM 495, a half block east off Sugar Road. He had also moved his second Lull house to a location just across the alley to the south of his business on 811 W Lee. Alvin rented the building, as well as the house, and when it became available, the services were conducted there after some remodeling was done.

The first Mennonite Brethren service in Pharr was held on March 23, 1969, with 34 in Sunday school, most of whom had come from McAllen. Until the summer of 1973, all services were conducted in Spanish.

The first person to serve in an English Mennonite Brethren group in the Pharr LAMB church was Tim Kliewer from Ulysses, Kansas. Tim and Myrna Nickel Kliewer had worked at El Faro and Los Ebanos from 1961 to 1963 and had also served in a new church in Denver, Colorado. As a member of the U.S. Conference Contemporary Concerns Committee, he served as liason between the U.S. Conference and the minority conferences in South Texas (Spanish) and in North Carolina (Blacks). This brought him back to the Valley several times. Tim wrote to Alvin Neufeld about serving in a church and he was invited to return. The Lord had laid it on his heart to return and work with the people he and his wife had learned to love ten years earlier.

In August, 1973, the Kliewers moved back with Timothy and Lois Jane. He went to work for Community Service System, a Denver-based public relations firm that expanded its services all over the United States. Three days after the Kliewers had moved to the Valley, Alvin Neufeld called on them and asked if they would be willing to consider having an early English service in the little church in Pharr on W 813 FM 495. A group of interested people met the following week and two weeks later they held the first English Mennonite Brethren service at 9:00 a.m. Sunday morning, September 9, 1973. Tim then visited with Zeral Brown and felt the time was right for a bilingual group to purchase the empty church on 413 North Sugar Road. Alvin Neufeld had also spoken to him about this, without realizing that Tim had done the same.

The time was right; a number of English-speaking Mennonite Brethren had moved to the Rio Grande Valley and various others spent parts of their winters there.

The place soon became too small with the two English and Spanish groups, so they gathered funds and built an educational addition during 1973. The church chartered on October 28, 1973; on the day of dedication 22 members signed the charter. On March 10, 1974, the Pharr building with the Sunday school addition was dedicated. It was a great occasion, since the day also featured the ordination of Tim Kliewer to the ministry.

The church, located on W 813 FM 495, was the first of its kind in the LAMB Conference, and this bilingual church was named Open Bible Mennonite Brethren Church. The first council consisted of: Alvin H. Neufeld, Spanish pastor and Moderator; Tim Kliewer, English pastor and member; Ruben Wedel, Secretary and Treasurer; Joe Suderman, member; Altagracia Villarreal, member.

The church advertised in the Mennonite Weekly Review, announcing its English-speaking Mennonite Brethren church service. Winter Texans began to come and room was desperately needed soon.

Zeral Brown had offered the vacant Pharr Bible Church on 413 N. Sugar Road to Alvin Neufeld. The Pharr Mennonite Brethren group took pledges to see if they could buy it, and found it was possible to make this great venture.

Pete Willems looked at the church and the little house on the property and recommended that the Board of Trustees of the Mennonite Brethren loan the entire sum to pay Zeral Brown. The vision of buying the Pharr Bible Church building and grounds became a reality on January 1, 1975; on the next day, January 2, the first services were held by Mennonite Brethren in that church.

Through the years the Pharr Church has attracted Canadian and American Mennonite winter visitors from Mennonite Brethren, General Conference, Old Mennonite and some Conservative Amish churches. Since Pharr is the only English-speaking Mennonite church in the Valley, it provides a real need for fellowship for visiting Mennonites.

These Winter Texans are a real blessing to the church, giving generously and working at anything that needs to be done.

One of the early improvements was to buy used oak pews to fill the chapel, so that the metal chairs were free to be used where needed.

More and more Winter Texans came to hear Tim Kliewer preach and soon the Anglos far outnumbered the Spanish. Many of various Mennonite groups had found a winter church home at Pharr. They also heard Pastor Ben H. Wedel during the winter.

The Tim Kliewers left for Saloam Springs, Arkansas, February, 1979, and the Ben Wedels became bilingual pastor in June of that year.

D. THE WORK OF THE PHARR BILINGUAL MENNONITE BRETHREN CHURCH

While the church worshipped in the little chapel on W 813 FM 495, the English services were held at 9:00 a.m., followed by a short union service called Body Life. This was a time when anyone could share a testimony, make a prayer request or share an announcement. After that all went to the Sunday school classes in English or Spanish, an arrangement that worked for some years.

The pattern continued after Ben and Frances Wedel arrived. In 1982 all three services, the English, Spanish and Children's Church, began at 9:30 a.m., with the English service meeting in the sanctuary, the Spanish in the Social Hall and the Children's Church upstairs.

During the Body Life time, everything was said in English and Spanish, forming a bond which held the two groups together. This service was dropped in summer, 1984. During that same summer the church voted to have the Sunday school before the service.

Each group sings as long as it chooses before the sermon and has special numbers. There are usually language students from RGBI assigned to attend the Spanish services. Some of those also serve in singing and playing instruments.

E. WORK AMONG CHILDREN AND YOUTH IN MCALLEN-PHARR CHURCH

During the mid-sixties Alvin Neufeld and Ruben Wedel began a Christian Service Brigade Club for boys in the house on Maple Avenue while Ruth Neufeld and Eva Wedel had a Pioneer Girls Club in the Neufeld home. After the church moved to Pharr, Duane Gibson, a student at Rio Grande Language School, helped Alvin with the boys. There were Vacation Bible schools for the children from McAllen and also from Pharr. One year Henry and Anna Esau, with the help of Mr. and Mrs. Jerry Warkentin, conducted a Bible school at night during October in the church on W FM 495. It was well attended. After the congregation moved to the church on Sugar Road in 1972, there generally were Bible schools with children from McAllen and Pharr.

During school time in 1981-83, Michelle Whaley from Eugene, Oregon, a Christian Service worker, was responsible for the club work with girls. There were two clubs, one for the younger and another for older girls, which met on Wednesday nights in the educational wing. The first year they were Pioneer Clubs, and the second, Christian Girls Clubs. Other workers were Ruth Neufeld, Carol Stevens, Louise Esau, Blanca Flores and Anna Esau.

David Stevens and Juan Diego Flores began a boys club in 1982. After David left for Arkansas, Ben Wedel helped until later Michelle Whaley took over the CYF work with the youth. When she left in August, 1984, Mr. and Mrs. Ken Lochhead were elected in September, 1984.

F. THE EXTENSION WORK OF THE CHURCH

The Pharr church has members serving in many different places. They include Simón and Silvia Villarreal Perez, Nataniel and little Noelia, who work among the Zapoteco Indians in Oaxaca, Mexico;

Silvia's sister Benita and her husband Concepcion Diaz and three children, Isal, Elisema and Lida, in Santa Engracia, Tamaulipas, Mexico; and Lee and Shirley Mendoza, who operate Children's Haven International, which has its office in Pharr and the children's homes four miles west of Reynosa City along the highway to Monterrey. In 1984 they had six homes for over a hundred homeless children.

Pastor Ben Wedel has worked in the Edinburg County Jail with prisoners. Several have received the Lord and are studying the Bible. Ben and Francis Wedel did a great deal of visiting and also had Bible studies in homes.

G. THE PASTORS AND WORKERS OF THE MCALLEN-PHARR WORK

Alvin and Ruth Heidebrecht Neufeld left the village of Lull in 1963 and lived in two places in McAllen before moving to the Rio Grande Bible Institute in 1969 where he worked as a teacher and architect of a new building on campus. He kept up the pastorate, transportation of the McAllen members, as well as the radio work for the LAMB Conference until 1977. In July 1980, Alvin and Ruth moved to Camp Loma de Vida but kept up the church work.

Ruben and Eva Wiens Wedel were the pioneer missionaries of the La Grulla station. While working in the Pharr church they supported themselves by teaching. After Ruben retired from teaching they went to cook for the Bible Academy at Corn, Oklahoma. After two years there they moved to Cordel, Oklahoma. Eva died on April 28, 1984.

The Alfred H. Quirings from Canada came to RGBI to learn Spanish to serve the Lord in South America. When he became sick in 1967 they were assigned to help the group at McAllen doing visitation work. They returned to Canada when he could not take the semi-tropical climate of the Valley.

Yolanda Villarreal, a member of La Grulla Church, was employed by the Conference in 1964 to help at McAllen. She was especially gifted to work with children as well as adults.

Annie E. Dyck, from the Mennonite Brethren Church at Winkler, Manitoba, Canada, also helped along. She went to Colombia in January, 1946, where she served for several terms.

During the summer months, Alejandro Martinez helped in the McAllen Bible School. He attended Rio Grande Bible Institute the rest of the year.

Tim and Myrna Nickel Kliewer had served in El Faro and the Los Ebanos church 1961-63. In 1963 they left for California where she entered nurses training and he received his Masters of Divinity degree from the Mennonite Brethren Biblical Seminary in Fresno. They worked in Denver in church planting until 1973, when they moved to the Valley to a country home near Donna. They supported themselves and served in the first English Mennonite Brethren group in the LAMB Conference. The Kliewers served until the end of January,

1979, when they left to accept the pastorate of Siloam Springs Mennonite Brethren Church in Arkansas.

Ben H. and Frances Ediger Wedel came in June of 1979 from Marshal, Arkansas, with their sons Tim and Steve, while Sharon remained in Arkansas to finish college. Their daughter Carol and husband David Stevens also came to help in the church. The Stevens returned to Marshal in 1981.

Ben Wedel originally came from Collinsville, Oklahoma church and Frances from the church in Enid, Oklahoma. They both attended the Rio Grande Bible Institute and were married in the Lull Mennonite Brethren Church where Alvin Neufeld was the missionary. The Wedels served in Mexican Missions Ministries around Montclova, Mexico, for sixteen years before taking the family to Marshal, Arkansas, where he pastored in Mennonite Brethren churches. On December 4, 1983, he resigned the Pharr church but served until the 26th of February, when they were given a farewell. They have since moved to the church at Burlington, Colorado.

Tom B. and Linda Adams Haughey with Dawn came to serve as interim pastor until October 1, 1984. He works at the FM 97 KVMV radio station part-time and is the author of a number of books. They came from the Missionary Alliance Church and were received as members of the Pharr Mennonite Brethren congregation on June 3, 1984. Tom, a native of Washington, D.C., holds a Masters Degree in theology and was installed February 17, 1985.

The Mennonite Brethren Bible Church, as it had been renamed, elected Kenneth L. Esau as its first deacon in October, 1980.

During 1978 Sandy Penner and Laurel Derksen from Denver, Colorado, came as Christian workers for two years. Sandy taught and Laurel worked in a hospital laboratory. Michelle Whaley from Eugene, Oregon, came as a Christian Service worker in 1981. She found a job in an office to support herself. She helped by playing the piano and teaching and leading the clubs and the youth until September, 1984.

CHAPTER 13

THE MENNONITE BRETHREN CHURCH AT DONNA

A. THE TOWN OF DONNA, TEXAS

Donna lies mostly on the south side of Expressway 83, about ten miles east of McAllen, with Pharr, San Juan and Alamo in between. It has its own school district and its own high school and is a thriving town.

B. EARLY GOSPEL EFFORTS IN DONNA

M.C. Ehlert also came to Donna, set up his gospel tent and preached to whoever would come. People were saved in Donna and Ehlert baptized them and formed a small congregation. A brick church was built on 2209 Benites Avenue in the eastern part of Donna. After Ehlert's evangelistic campaigns had resulted in several small congregations, he acquired land in the south part of Edinburg and began the Rio Grande Bible Institute. At first the courses were in English to train missionaries; a complete Spanish Bible course was later introduced. These students were sent out to the various churches that Ehlert had founded as well as others.

Whenever possible, a couple was placed in Donna to work with the people when the student pastor was not in school. In 1966 this church in Donna was offered to the Latin American Mennonite Brethren Conference for $2,000. The Donna congregation borrowed the money and paid the Rio Grande Bible Institute and later paid off the loan.

C. THE DONNA MENNONITE BRETHREN CHURCH

Enrique Galvan was a student pastor at Donna when the congregation bought the property from RGBI. Enrique and Julia Galvan were accepted as workers in the Latin American Mennonite Brethren Conference in 1966. They have one daughter, Juanita.

The church grew and, during the time Galvan was there, they added a baptistry, two small rooms, and also made improvements on the parsonage. Since the installation of H. Cornejo in 1981, the church has asked for funds to build some Sunday school rooms. They will rebuild what was added years ago and add to it. The new part is built of cement blocks and will add Sunday school rooms and a kitchen.

D. WORK AMONG THE YOUTH AND CHILDREN

During the time the Galvans served at Donna, they worked among the young people, leading a nice group. They took them to El Faro once a month for the CYF. They also tried to interest children in Bible school and asked Henry and Anna Esau to come conduct the Bible school. For three years the Esaus conducted the Bible school and children came to paint Spanish plaques.

Later, when Simón Rada served, Five Day Child Evangelism Bible schools were conducted for some years.

E. WORKERS AT THE DONNA MENNONITE BRETHREN CHURCH

Enrique Galvan is a native of the Valley who married and went to California to work. Although he had grown up in the Methodist Church, he had never accepted the Lord and lived a worldly life. Juanita began to attend Sunday school and was saved, as was her mother. Both were praying for Enrique until he finally accepted Christ. He felt called to served the Lord and came to the Rio Grande Bible Institute. It was difficult for him, since he had been a school drop-out, but he worked hard and, with God's grace, graduated.

Enrique is a very good evangelist with a powerful delivery. He served on the Administrative Committee as well as evangelist in several churches. He was ordained on February 18, 1967. The Galvans left for California in June, 1968.

Simón Rada was a member of the Donna Mennonite Brethren church when he felt called to serve the Lord. Then when the Galvans left in 1967, Simón, a student at RGBI, was asked to be student pastor. Simón and Marta Rada served for some time after he finished his studies. They left with Josie and Rogelio for Davenport, Iowa, where he pastors a Mennonite church.

After the Radas left, various RGBI groups came to preach, sing, or teach. In 1972, Rafael Plazola served until June. Jonas Ybarra took charge and Alvin Neufeld came to help until Anselmo Salinas went to preach at Donna.

In 1974, John Carpenter went to Donna, and Paul Castillo went as a student. Paul Castillo was a native of Mission and member and worker in the church. Castillo became a member of LAMB Educational Board while a student, preaching at Donna while he attended RGBI for three years. He then became pastor of the La Grulla church in September, 1977. Anselmo Salinas also worked in Donna from 1976-77. Various students again served at Donna until August, 1980, when John Wall, also a student at RGBI, began to preach at Donna. John served until May, 1981, when he married Becky Neufeld and they went to work in Spain during the summer. After that they took the pastorate of the Mission Mennonite Brethren Church. Herculano Cornejo was licensed by LAMB and installed as pastor in May, 1981. He and his wife Matilda live in Donna.

CHAPTER 14

THE LATIN AMERICAN MENNONITE BRETHREN CONFERENCE IN TEXAS

I.
THE WORK OF THE PROVISIONAL LATIN AMERICAN MENNONITE BRETHREN CONFERENCE

A. THE WORK OF SETTING UP A CONFERENCE ADMINISTRATIVE COMMITTEE

The churches of Los Ebanos, Chihuahua, La Grulla, La Joya, Mission, Garciasville, Lull, and Premont had all been missions and the Southern District Conference had supported the missionaries and built the chapels except for Lull (Edinburg). By 1948, there was a council composed of the missionaries of the churches, except those of Premont. This board was mostly occupied with El Faro School. The missionaries often met for fellowship and spiritual inspiration, but not as a conference.

When the work had grown so large that the Southern District could no longer continue to pay the bills and also build new churches, the work of the Southern District Mennonite Brethren Conference was given to the Mennonite Brethren Foreign Mission Board.

To implement a provisional conference, A.E. Janzen and John Ratzlaff, members of the Foreign Mission Board from Hillsboro, Kansas, came to Texas in January, 1960. The missionaries had been asked to choose delegates to vote for a committee which was to provide the beginnings of the organization of the Latin American Mennonite Brethren Conference. On January 7, 1960, the missionaries and members of their churches met at El Faro School. A.E. Janzen explained how a conference functioned and Ricardo Peña translated it into Spanish. At this conference, a committee was elected to prepare a working basis as well as provide a charter and a constitution.

On January 8, 1960, A.E. Janzen met with Ricardo Peña, Alfredo Tagle, Eugene Janzen, Dan Wirsche and Inocencio Garcia to organize the Administrative Committee which had been elected the day before. A.E. Janzen led this meeting until Alfredo Tagle was chosen as chairman. Ricardo Peña was elected as secretary-treasurer, and Inocencio Garcia as assistant chairman. Dan Wirsche and Eugene Janzen were chosen as members.

B. THE WORK OF THE PROVISIONAL TRUSTEE BOARD

Before chartering the conference, a Board of Trustees was required; the Administrative Committee set up a mini-conference to hold an election to choose six directors.

On February 4, 1960, at a meeting at El Faro School, eighteen delegates met to elect the six trustees. Those elected were Alvin Neufeld (chairman), Juan Noyola (assistant chairman), Leonel Saenz (secretary-treasurer), Ricardo Peña, Inocencio Garcia and Federico Pena.

Since Alvin Neufeld had incorporated the Lull Church, he wrote the constitution for the Latin American Mennonite Brethren. It was explained, amended and accepted by the Trustees at the meetings of the committee.

II.
THE WORK OF THE
LATIN AMERICAN
MENNONITE BRETHREN CONFERENCE

A. THE ORGANIZATION OF THE LATIN AMERICAN MENNONITE BRETHREN CONFERENCE

Three years had passed since the Provisional Administrative Committee had been formed in January, 1960. The committee had notified all the churches and each one elected delegates, one for each ten members. The pastors were all delegates. The first business conference of all the churches was held at El Faro on February 16, 1960. For the first time they elected three important groups to do the work of the conference. Alfredo Tagle was chairman of the Provisional Committee.

At that time the Educational Board was called El Faro School Board. The conference elected five people to look after the welfare of the school: Leonel Saenz, Ricardo Peña, Antonio Garcia, Juan Noyola, and Abelardo Mireles Jr.

The next important item was the election of a new Administrative Committee: Dan A. Wirsche, Alvin H. Neufeld, Henry Boese, Octavio Cantu, and Alejandro Martinez.

The Board of Trustees had done a great deal of work so the conference voted by acclamation that Alvin Neufeld, Ricardo Peña, Juan Noyola, Inocencio Garcia, and Leonel Saenz be kept to serve on the new board; Henry T. Esau was elected as the sixth member.

At the first meeting of the newly elected Administrative Committee on March 9, 1963, Dan A. Wirsche presided and the group decided that the election of three Anglos and two Latins (Mexican Americans) was not a good choice. They set a new day for the same delegates to have another election for members of the Administrative Committee. The following served in 1963: Inocencio Garcia as chairman, Alvin Neufeld as vice-chairman and secretary, Juan Cortez, Daniel A.

Wirsche, and Juan Noyola. In 1964 they were Inocencio Garcia, Alfredo Tagle, Alvin Neufeld, Antonio Garcia, Daniel A. Wirsche, and Federico Garcia, with Inocencio Garcia as chairman. In 1967 the members were I. Garcia, Jonas Ybarra, Ruben Wedel, E. Galvan, Frank Muñoz and Alvin Neufeld. The conference of 1964 requested that each church ratify the constitution. This was to be done in the month of September of the same year.

At times the Administrative Committee met with the Educational Board to decide how to spend the money sent by the Foreign Mission Board for the workers and the Southern District for El Faro. The Texas Commission from the conference sent to help LAMB were P.J. Funk, E. Karber and, later, R. Vogt and H.R. Wiens.

The Administrative Committee has been serving for several other committees such as Reference and Counsel, Ministerial, Program Committee and Home Missions. A new Board for Missions was chosen in 1976 and 1977.

B. WORK DONE IN LAMB CONFERENCE, INCLUDING YOUTH AND CHILDREN

The business conference first met in January or February of each year. Then, in 1966, there were two conferences, the second in November to change to a year beginning October 1st and ending September 30th.

After that change there usually was a Bible or a Missionary Conference in March in which the youth and children had separate services. As long as El Faro belonged to the conference, the March Youth Conference was held there at the same time the adults met. The groups all met together in the El Faro Auditorium for the last service.

After the El Faro school was closed in 1969, the conferences were held in the churches.

The youth organization was made a standing committee by the LAMB conference of 1967. This committee, according to the revised constitution, has seven members. Two are elected by the conference delegation and five by the Christian Youth Fellowship (CYF). Those chosen organize after each annual election. The young people have their own election just before the annual conference.

In some of the churches they have a CYF meeting each Friday or Saturday night; all the CYF groups meet once a month in one of the churches. In this way the young folks learn to know those of the various churches.

The first group to travel was nine young folks taken by Alvin Neufeld. They attended "Explo '72" during June 12 to 17. That time the Southern District Home Mission Board and several churches gave offerings to pay for the trip. Later Alvin Neufeld took the group to various churches to do visitation work and give a program at night.

A good number went in 1979 to the Estes Retreat arranged by the

U.S. Area Christian Education Board and the Estes Planning Committee.

Rolando Mireles from the La Grulla church was one of the members of the Planning Committee for the 1983 retreat. A group of about seventy went to Estes '83 in spring. Their sponsors were Wesley and Zita Wirsche from La Joya, Rudolfo and Adela Peña, and John and Becky Wall from Mission. Several saw snow for the first time in their lives.

There are organizations among young people that serve in various churches such as "Caros de Dios," "Chariots of God," a band led by Moises (Moy) Tagle. By 1984 the different members were busy at other things so there was no more time to practice. Moises then began to direct a LAMB Choir coming from different churches. During the early eighties they performed at the various conferences.

C. RADIO WORK DONE BY THE LAMB CONFERENCE

Interest in radio work began early in the 60s. In a meeting on January 22, 1964, it was decided to try to get on the station covering much of Mexico and all of the Valley. The proposition was presented at the Conference of February 28 to March 1, 1964, and the Mennonite Brethren program began in 1964 and continued to 1977. It was paid for by the Latin American Churches.

"La Fuente Viva," or "The Living Fountain," went on the air for the first time on June 21, 1964, from XERKS Reynosa, Tamaulipas, Mexico. Around a year later another station in Ciudad Miguel Aleman, Tamaulipas took the program. Stations XEHI and XEWD also had it on for a short time. Due to lack of interest in the churches, the program was dropped for eighteen months, before beginning again in fall, 1969, when interest was revived and Alfredo Tagle was elected by the conference to be the radio pastor with Jonas Ybarra as announcer. Before that, the pastors took turns giving the messages. In 1970, Pedro Durik, then serving at Garciasville, was elected to be pastor of La Fuente Viva and the conference voted to go on KGBI at Harlingen, Texas. The first program went out on January 31, 1971. Durik moved to Indiana in January, but continued to send his sermons on tape for the rest of the year. On June 6, 1971, KSRT, Tracy, California, took the program as a public service. A children's program began on April 4, 1965, for XERK and in July for XGHI, with Yolanda Villarreal or Ofelia Tagle telling the story. The recording was done in the home of Alvin Neufeld. During the last years, the programs were recorded at the church in Pharr.

After 1977, the program was no longer produced. Rolando and Lucila Mireles completed the correspondence courses that children and others were still working on.

During the later years, La Fuente Viva used good quality music for its programming, much of it coming from HCJB, Quito, Ecuador.

La Fuente Viva was a missionary evangelistic outreach. The conference report of October, 1972, shows that seven churches supported the program and have given to it, while only $23.91 came from radio listeners.

Besides the cost of the tapes and airing of the program, La Fuente Viva gave out tracts, calendars, correspondence courses, testaments and Bibles.

D. THE LAMB MISSION WORK

1. The Outreach to Mexico by the Mission Churches

Alfredo Villarreal was saved at Los Ebanos. While attending the Rio Grande Bible Institute in 1950, he received a burden to share the gospel with his relatives and others in Mexico. He crossed the Rio Grande River at Los Ebanos each weekend, going first to the villages of Agruelles and Venecia. The Harry Neufelds went to visit his congregation, which gathered under a portal (a temporary roof), or in a house.

In 1954, Alfredo started services in San Miguel, now Diaz Ordaz; in 1956 Alfredo and Raquel were accepted by the Foreign Mission Board as missionaries.

In 1959 Alfredo and Raquel received help to build a church when German and Bertha Contreras, with son Jonatan, came from the Mennonite Brethren Mission at Nuevo Ideal in Durango, Mexico. They built a large brick church and the two couples served together for around three years before Alfredo and Raquel went to work for Mexican Missions Ministries at Montclova. They left with David, Samuel, Ruth and Rebeca.

German and Bertha Contreras stayed at San Miguel, working after support from the Foreign Mission was ended. The LAMB Conference decided to help the church, in what is now called Diaz Ordaz, which has grown and is reaching out to other places. In 1984 the Contreras lived in the old Los Ebanos parsonage so the children, several American-born, could attend school in the U.S.

Another church was begun in Reynosa, Mexico during the early 60s among poor people. They began by trying to grow gardens to help them survive. Victor Gonzales, a young man from the area, took charge of services and Alvin Neufeld visited the group on Sunday afternoons. The believers built the adobe walls for a church and waited for money to put on a roof. Heavy rains damaged the walls and the church was never finished. Victor Gonzales was accepted by the Foreign Mission Board and sent to another place in Mexico; his brother Leoncio took charge at Reynosa, but when he was killed in a car wreck, the group was left to itself and the Lord.

2. The Work of LAMB Mission Board

The LAMB Conference of November 3, 1976, held at Garciasville, elected a Mission Committee consisting of Inocencio Garcia, Joe Suderman, Alvin Neufeld and Alfredo Tagle, who investigated the possibility of beginning mission work in Mexico. The next conference, in 1977, added two more members, Ricardo Peña and Tim Kliewer; they called themselves the Board of Missions and Evangelism. The newly organized board had its eyes on the city of Reynosa, a city of 200,000, across the river from Hidalgo, south of McAllen. The city has greatly changed since the time our first missionaries saw it. Then the streets were dirt gutters when it rained and dust bowls when it was dry. Now the streets are paved, the city has electricity and the merchants mostly speak English and have their feast days on American holidays to attract trade. Very many tourists visit Reynosa.

The Board prayed and searched for the right persons for Reynosa, contacting various pastors. Valente Hernandez highly recommended Carlos and Emma Roman and, after interviewing them, the Board presented them to the conference of 1977. The Romans gave their testimony and expressed their desire to work with the Mennonite Brethren and were accepted.

Carlos Roman, as a young man, was an alcoholic. During one drunken binge he got into a brawl and was jailed in Sonora state, below Arizona. Some young people visited the jail, bringing songs and a gospel message, inviting Roman to come to church when he was released. Carlos told God, "If You can change me the way these young people say You can, then I want to serve You." He accepted Christ as Savior, attended seminary in La Puente, California, and held several pastorates in Mexico. Carlos and Emma de Leon Roman came to Reynosa with Carlos Armando in 1977.

Since it was a pioneer work, they did a great deal of visiting, giving the gospel and inviting people to come for services which were held in their home. They crowded together in a few rooms, leaving the larger rooms of the house for the services and Sunday school. During 1982, 40 to 50 persons, mostly new Christians, attended services.

From the beginning of the work in Reynosa, Ricardo Peña went to help on Sunday nights. In the morning Yolanda Villarreal went to teach the children. As more and more came, Mrs. Carmen Peña, sister of Yolanda, also went to teach the older children. Emma Roman did what she could to interest mothers in the gospel and give them God's Word. Later, Jessie and Dina Peña Medina also went to help. Ten persons were baptized during the stay of Carlos Roman.

When the house became too small, the Mission Board purchased a church that had been started by workers of BEMA Mission, located about five miles on Matamoras Road in a new addition called Colonia Juarez. The church building in Colonia Juarez lies northeast of Reynosa center and is about five miles from where the first work was started. The groups were merged and a third small congregation, started by Arthur and Helen Dalke, has been added. In 1983 the congregation began to build an addition to the existing building.

Carlos and Emma Roman left Reynosa with Carlos Armando and Jessica in September, 1982, to pastor the church La Iglesia de Gracia at Garciasville, Texas.

After the Romans left, Miguel de Leon came from Monterrey. He is a graduate of Seminario Biblico and licensed to preach in Mexico.

Yolanda Villarreal, Mr. and Mrs. Ricardo Peña and others helped him in the work.

The work in Diaz Ordaz, begun in 1954 by Alfredo Villarreal, was continued by German Contreras and survived through the years. The family had grown to include Jonatan, Eunice, David, Josue, Laura, Azael, Rebeca, and Heftali. A number of former members of Diaz Ordaz joined the Pharr church and, in time, the Pharr congregation became involved. The Diaz Ordaz Mennonite Brethren Church was also accepted as a LAMB mission and is receiving help.

Reynosa and Diaz Ordaz are two places where the LAMB Conference did mission work. In 1982 the budget was $10,000 a year and represents the largest single combined effort of the conference. Both of the Mexican churches are expected to help pay part of the pastors' salaries and continue as they are able.

In 1983 another work was accepted; located not far from the city of Lineras, Tamaulipas, Mexico, it was begun by Inev Cabrera, a member of the Mission Mennonite Brethren Church who originally came from a place near Magueyes. She and her mother, Franscisca, were concerned that their own people had no one to witness to them. In summer, 1980, Yolanda Villarreal and Inez Cabrera went to conduct Bible schools in various places. In spring, 1984, Inez and her brother, Angel, went to teach Bible school. Yolanda joined them later to work with the women. Several women have been saved, as have some men. Some of the leaders of the village and the workers are anxious to see these people get a church.

E. VARIOUS OTHER ACTIVITIES OF THE LAMB CONFERENCE

The Administrative Committee finds speakers for the annual Bible Conference, which usually convenes in March. Since El Faro no longer belongs to the conference, the meetings are held in different churches. Each church has its regular morning service and then comes to the Bible Conference in the afternoon. The conference is also occasionally held in one of the many parks. The churches each bring food for a supper and then all stay for another service. The Missions Conference in September is run much in the same way.

During the seventies, when Ruben Wedel was chairman, the Board of Education held a conference-wide Children's Day. Each church prepared some numbers and brought the children to present a program. The attendance usually was quite good for many parents brought their children. Children's Day usually is somewhere in between the other conferences.

For years the annual Business Conference met at night during the first days of November in different churches, giving members a chance to take part. The 1981, 1982, 1983 and 1984 conferences met at Camp Loma de Vida, located nine miles north of Edinburg on U.S. Highway 281.

For a number of years during the 60s the pastors and workers of the churches gathered for a supper and a program at either the McAllen or Mission Fireman's Park.

For a few years during the late 60s in summer there were retreats held at the Bible Academy at La Feria, Texas. The missionaries, church workers, and El Faro School staff sang and prayed together or listened to a message. The various boards held their business meetings in between sessions.

F. THE WOMEN'S MISSIONARY FELLOWSHIP

From the early years of the work all of the mission stations had many more women than men. There was a strong Bible study movement in the early churches among women, especially in Chihuahua. After the Harry Neufelds left, Mrs. Ruth Thomas felt it was time to unite the work of the various women's groups to form a fellowship called "Sociedad Feminil Misionera".

In 1961, the women's groups were called together at Garciasville and held their first election, choosing Emma Mireles from Los Ebanos as the first president. She served three years before Eloisa Cantu from La Grulla was elected. Mrs. Ofelia Tagle from Los Ebanos and La Joya served two different terms of three years; various others have held the position and served well, among them Guadalupe Vargas from the Pharr church.

The Women's Missionary Fellowship meets twice a year in spring just before the Missionary Conference, which used to convene for a supper and a program. In several of the churches the women made various things such as quilts, aprons, fancy work, to sell at meetings.

There is special music from the various churches, a testimony meeting and a speaker, often one invited from some other church or organization. The programs vary and there may be a number participating to carry out the conference theme.

Each year the Women's Missionary Fellowship gives a report to the fall conference of the work and the projects the women have undertaken. As long as El Faro was in operation, they did what they could to help the school. Now the one concern all have in common are the conference missions, or students in RGBI, who need some help.

G. THE MEN'S FELLOWSHIP

Inocencio Garcia recalls that during the years that missionaries Neufeld, Thomas and Wedel were on the field, they held meetings with men from the stations. They met for fellowship and prayer, but never formed an organization with officers responsible for various functions.

The November, 1966, conference decided to form a Men's Fellowship called "Sociedad Varonil," and instructed the Administrative Committee to seek means and methods to carry out the plans.

The Administrative Committee minutes for February 10, 1967, recorded that 21 met for a supper at Central Power and Light Park. Anselmo Salinas, president, Jonas Ybarra, vice-president, Inez Ybarra, secretary, and Antonio Garcia, treasurer, decided that the Men's Fellowship was to meet on the second Saturday of each month.

On May 28, 1976, at Garciasville, the first Men's Breakfast was held; Inocencio Garcia inspired the men of the conference to meet for a breakfast the last Sunday of each month. Garcia became its first chairman, Domingo Villarreal the second and Rudolfo Peña the third in 1983. The men cook their own breakfast in whatever church they meet and have Christian fellowship and collect money for conference projects. Some twenty to thirty come for the breakfast.

H. THE WORK OF THE CHRISTIAN EDUCATION BOARD

During the early years, the Administrative Committee of the missionaries also did the educational work. After the founding of El Faro, there was a school board composed of the missionaries, Harry Neufeld, Henry Thomas, Ruben Wedel and Ricardo Peña which directed Christian education, using the teachers to help in various ways. The El Faro teachers all served teaching Summer Bible schools in the various churches, using Scripture Press materials. During 1973, while Henry Esau was chairman of the Educational Board, there was very little material on hand so he and Anna worked weeks to prepare materials which they ran on their duplicator and Mrs. Tomasa Cruz of the Garciasville church duplicated many pictures to be colored. Each church had to provide its own craft for the school.

In 1972, the Educational Board invited the Valley Child Evangelism workers, Mr. and Mrs. Charles Swett to conduct training sessions to better qualify Sunday school teachers.

One year the Board also arranged for a training school that met on six Friday nights in the Mission church. Anselmo Salinas taught the history of the Sunday school movement and the Esaus taught a class on how to teach various age groups.

After Ruben Wedel became chairman of the board, the teachers were encouraged to prepare special numbers from each church and give a special Children's Day program. This gave the teachers and pupils an incentive to learn Bible verses and songs to render at the program.

For some time during the seventies, the Educational Board decided to publish a newsletter named LAMB News. People sent news items to Henry T. Esau; on the way to Garciasville, he took the copies to reach the churches by Sunday. For some time Anselmo Salinas also did the work.

In 1982 the board sponsored a teachers' workshop at La Joya Church. Ofelia Tagle taught about visual aids, Yolanda Villarreal showed teachers how to win pupils for the Lord and Anna Esau taught teachers how to study to become better instructors.

I. THE COMMITTEE OF GENERAL WELFARE AND MENNO-NITE DISASTER SERVICE

The Conference of 1972 elected five members to begin to serve in close coordination with Mennonite Disaster Service. Inocencio Garcia presented this phase of mission work and became the first chairman of the committee. Others who served were Ricardo Peña, Antonio Garcia and Alberto Sanchez. They helped some victims during hurricane Beulah and, when the Children's Haven burned in Reynosa, collected clothing from the churches and gave it to the orphans and others living there.

J. LEADERS OF LAMB CONFERENCE

1. Ricardo R. Peña, one of the first converts from Los Ebanos, became the first native accepted as a missionary by the Home Missions Committee of the Southern District. He served while still a youth in various outreach locations such as Havana, Premont, Garciasville and La Joya. The conference ordained him on March 7, 1954.

Ricardo was the first Mexican American on the El Faro School Board in 1948, and the only one who served until it was closed in 1969.

Ricardo and Carmen pastored the La Joya church, which they began. They also served the Chihuahua church about a year. They later moved to Mission in 1960 and worked there until 1977, staying in the same church longer than any one other native pastor. Ricardo grew up with the conference and helped shape it. After the LAMB mission opened in Reynosa, the Peñas went to help, supporting themselves as Ricardo carried mail, at first only as a substitute, and later as a carrier for Route 3 in Mission, Texas. He did the church work at nights and days he had free.

2. Inocencio Garcia, one of a family led of the Lord to settle on a ranch called Chihuahua, prayed for a church. Harry Neufeld was the first one to visit in that area and the first convert baptized by Harry Neufeld was Marta Espinoza, an aunt of Inocencio Garcia, who lived in the village of Abram. Inocencio and Amelia were among those who helped form the Chihuahua church; he soon became Harry Neufeld's helper. He later served as assistant pastor, together with Henry Thomas, before going to Mission, Texas. Garcia also was on that first elected Administrative Committee that called the first conference.

Inocencio Garcia was elected to be one of the first trustees and his name appears on the charter as the initial registered agent of the corporation. By 1983, Garcia still says, "Our biggest need is money. We have the vision and maturity, but no money." He sees how much could and should be done but also sees the problems. He is pushing for a work to begin in McAllen. He, like Alfredo Tagle, has served on U.S. conference boards and committees.

Inocencio Garcia was elected moderator of the first Administrative

Committee by the first LAMB Conference held in 1963, a position he held until 1969.

The family moved to Lull in 1964 and stayed until Amelia became very ill. Meanwhile the structure which had been built on Garcia's lots was dismantled to become a part of La Joya church. Inocencio built a house on the Chihuahua church floor. While they lived there, Amelia died on August 5, 1974.

Later Inocencio Garcia married Mrs. Oralia Hernandez, a teacher from McAllen. Together they served at Garciasville after Henry T. Esau became too ill to continue. They stayed until Inocencio had a heart attack and had to take time off for rest. By July, 1983 he was recovered enough to take the La Joya church. To be able to devote all of his strength to the church, Garcia resigned his conference offices. In 1984 he began gathering people living in Chihuahua and has services with them.

3. Alfredo Tagle, a native of Lull, two miles north of Edinburg, was one of the first converts of Alvin Neufeld. During the early 1950s he attended Rio Grande Bible Institute; in summers he worked as a truck driver and migrant worker. Like many others, he followed the vegetable harvest during the day and preached in the migrant camps by night.

When Alvin Neufeld told Alfredo of an opening in the Los Ebanos church, he gladly took the opportunity to preach the gospel even though the financial sacrifice was enormous. Tagle recalls, "I didn't live, I just existed." He worked there as a single man until the missionaries were able to take over. This sacrifice has continued through the years; the La Joya church gave him only $300 a month. To educate four children, he worked as a cabinet maker while Ofelia, his wife, also worked in a headstart school and later in a migrant teaching program.

Tagle, like Ricardo Peña and Inocencio Garcia, helped guide the emerging LAMB Conference.

Alfredo Tagle was chairman of the first Administrative Committee elected when A.E. Janzen came to Texas in January, 1960. He served as chairman until the election held at the first conference, early in 1963.

Alfredo Tagle, with his bride, was sent to the Southern District Conference, where he preached an English sermon. The missionaries, praying as he preached, clearly understood that the mission work among the Mexican Americans had not been in vain. In October, 1960, Tagle was sent to the conference at Reedley, California; he currently serves as a member of the U.S. Conference Board of Church ministries (BCM). Alfredo has seen LAMB grow from its beginnings to a well-organized and properly led conference, and he takes pride in this accomplishment. He used to feel the Latin Americans were only followers while the missionaries did the planning, but now he says, "We can think for ourselves." He is a member of the LAMB Mission Board which is in charge of the Reynosa and Diaz Ordaz missions.

4. Alvin and Ruth Neufeld have supported themselves through the years. They say, "We just praise the Lord for how He can make a little support do an awful lot."

During the 1950s, while still studying at the Rio Grande Bible Institute, the Neufelds moved their travel trailer to Lull, two miles north of Edinburg, and began to give the gospel to Mexican Americans living in that village. They served there for twelve years.

By 1960 there was no one who had more experience and knowledge on how to write a charter and a constitution than Alvin, so he did the major share of the work and his name is also on the charter.

To help support his family of five children, Alvin set up a water softening business while still living at Lull. At first he worked from a rented building in McAllen, and later built his own on W 813 FM 495 in Pharr. This place became the church building for the first bilingual congregation in the LAMB Conference.

Alvin and Ruth also lived on the campus of the Rio Grande Bible Institute, where Alvin drew many of the plans for the new buildings of the Institute. Ruth taught many Institute students to play the piano during the years. In 1980 they moved to Camp Loma de Vida, which he helped establish some twenty years before. Now he has plans to expand the complex for both young and old and make it a year-round service.

From 1964-77, Alvin and Ruth also were responsible for "La Fuente Viva," a radio program supported by the LAMB Conference. One LAMB leader calls Neufeld, "one of the unsung heroes of the conference. He helped make the conference successful. He always cares about the work. You could always go to him if you had a problem or needed help. He would always find time for us." Neufeld resigned from the Administrative Committee and joined the newly formed LAMB Mission Board in 1976. He says, "You push a mission program, and you'll grow."

5. Henry T. and Anna Esau came to the Valley from the mission at Premont in 1960, and were there during the years LAMB was emerging as a conference. He was elected to fill the first opening on the original Board of Trustees and also on the El Faro School Board, serving as chairman much of the time until the closing of the school in 1969. After that, he continued to work to train better Sunday school teachers through workshops in each of the churches. He ordered the Vacation Bible school materials and also encouraged churches to use it at a time when they could reach the most children. Henry and Anna taught over thirty schools, furnishing the materials, the music, the missionary story and the craft. Children loved to paint gospel plaques. There were new ones each year.

Henry also was one of the founders of Camp Loma de Vida and served as vice-president as long as he was able. He and Anna also taught Bible and craft classes at camp.

Henry Esau taught eleven years in Lamar School in Edinburg. During this time he and Anna served in Lull for twelve years doing the educational work in Sunday school, mid-week school and the Bible school.

After Henry Esau retired from teaching, he took the pastorate at Iglesia de Gracia in Garciasville in September, 1972. Each weekend for nearly four years they spent a few days in the village working on the church or visiting. He became ill and had to retire to their home just across the street from Lamar School. He spent the last six months in a nursing home, where he died on January 31, 1980, the first Mennonite Brethren missionary to die on the field in Texas. The funeral was at the Pharr church and the workers and many of the conference people came on Saturday, February 2, to express their love for one who had served LAMB. Many were the testimonies of what he had meant to various people. He was buried on the family lot at Buhler, Kansas.

6. Ruben and Eva Wedel, early missionaries at La Grulla, returned to the Valley in 1960. They lived in Pharr and taught in various schools. After the Neufelds moved to McAllen, the Wedels went to help, where he served as assistant pastor and Sunday school superintendent. When the congregation moved to Pharr, Ruben and Eva Wedel continued to serve in various capacities in the church. Many of their summers were spent cooking for youth camps in Colorado.

Ruben also served the LAMB Conference on the Educational Board as chairman for some time. They returned to Oklahoma in 1981 to cook for the Corn Bible Academy for two years. They later sold their home in Pharr and moved to Cordel, Oklahoma to serve in the church there. He had a heart attack and Eva became ill so the building of a new home had to be postponed. Eva died suddenly on April 28, 1984.

7. Daniel A. and Elsie Wirsche were missionaries in Colombia and Mexico under the Mennonite Brethren Foreign Missions Board. They moved to McAllen, Texas in 1960 to help the fledgling LAMB Conference. He was on the provisional Administrative Committee that called a conference to elect a Board of Trustees who provided the charter and a constitution; he was also elected to the first official Administrative Committee. Wirsche took the Chihuahua church and became El Faro School superintendent from 1962-67; both taught in El Faro when and where they were needed. They left with Donald, their youngest son, to return to Uruguay, in March, 1968.

8. Jonas Ybarra was elected to the Administrative Committee by the Conference of 1966. A member of the Mennonite Brethren Church in Mission, Texas, Ybarra had attended Pacific College at Fresno, California. He was chosen as chairman of the Committee on November 18, 1966 and served until April 3, 1967 when he took the vice chairmanship. Inocencio Garcia finished the year as chairman. Jonas Ybarra married Lucille Gonzales and worked in the Donna Mennonite Brethren Church for some time.

9. Enrique and Julia Galvan pastored the Mennonite Brethren Church at Donna. He was chosen chairman of the Administrative Committee on November 27, 1967. Galvan served until June, 1968, when he and his wife moved to California.

10. Wesley Wirsche, son of Daniel A. Wirsche, and Antonio Garcia, the deacon of Chihuahua, took over the church when Daniel and Elsie left for Uruguay. Wesley was elected to the Administrative Committee in 1969 and was moderator of the conference from 1970 until 1978 when he became secretary. Wesley and Zita served in the merged La Joya church. While she worked in a doctor's office he taught in La Joya schools. Later they both taught. Wirsche speaks of "love" given by God as the key element of the LAMB Conference. He says, "You can go to any church in the conference and you immediately belong." Wesley and Zita would like to see an outreach for each church. "If you don't have an outreach program you're dead," he comments. Wirsche, referring to the conference, said, "We didn't see any real maturity until the money was cut off. We had been too dependent. It forced us to become self-sufficient."

11. Rolando Mireles, as grandson of Abelardo Mireles Sr., is a third generation Christian. He grew up in Los Ebanos, the first Mennonite Brethren mission station in Texas. Rolando heard the stories of the trials of his grandfather and says, "We have it soft now. In the old days it was much harder." When the mission stations suddenly found themselves on their own, it brought great concern. "How shall we make it?" many wondered. Progress was slow at first. Rolando says, "We didn't have any leaders of our own and for a few years it seemed like things were going downhill. We lost members, but then all those who really felt a love for the conference and the Lord's work here started surfacing. We had nobody telling us what to do anymore so we figured, 'Hey! We need to do it now!'"

Rolando and his wife Lucila live near her folks out on a ranch north of La Grulla. They both teach in the La Grulla schools and work in the church and in the conference. He became moderator in 1979, and serves at present (1984). Rolando also is a member of the Tabor College School Board.

He does not concern himself with deep doctrinal subjects but loves the Word and teaches and preaches when the need arises. He says, "We are trying to get through to our people that going to church is not enough; we want to get our people more enthused about actually doing the Lord's work." Rolando told the interviewers of the Christian Leader, "I love being at church. I'd rather be there than at home. I'd rather be there than at school."

12. Several other pastors and laymen, as well as some women, have held offices on conference boards. Ben Wedel was pastor of Pharr from June, 1979 to February 26, 1984.

Paul Castillo, a pastor of Donna and La Grulla until 1982, stressed Bible reading and memorization at La Grulla. He was elected to the Educational Board when still a student in school at Mission. He later attended and finished Rio Grande Bible Institute.

Anselmo Salinas also was a member of the Administrative Committee, Educational Board and pastor of various churches.

Juan Noyola from the Chihuahua church was assistant chairman on the Board of Trustees.

Leonel Saenz from the Garciasville church was on the El Faro School board, as well as secretary and treasurer of the Board of Trustees in 1960.

Federico Peña, father of Ricardo Peña from Los Ebanos, was a Trustee of the initial Board of Directors of LAMB Corporation.

Juan Cortez from the Chihuahua church was a member of the Administrative Committee until he moved to California.

Roberto Zamora from Mission is on the Board of Trustees.

Antonio Garcia and Federico Garcia were members of the Administrative Committee during the early years of the conference.

Manuel Guerra from Garciasville and Rodolfo Peña have served on the Tabor College Senate. In 1973 Kenneth L. Esau was elected.

Many more have served during the years. Among them are Ramon Flores, Crispin Diaz, John Wall, José Delgado, Herculano Cornejo, Kenneth L. Esau and Joe Suderman. "Dr. Joe," as he is known to the conference, served on the Mission Board, but did more by helping sick missionaries at half the cost or completely free. He operated a clinic together with his cousin, Dr. Emery Suderman. Dr. Joe, from Pharr church, operates a maternity ward and delivers around 600 babies a year.

Ruperto Villalon from the La Joya church was elected chairman of the Educational Board, and Frances Wedel, wife of Ben Wedel, was also elected. Other women are Mrs. Angelica Zamora, Mrs. Idalia G. Chapa, Elizabeth Tagle, Mrs. Gregoria Guerra, Alma Bazan, Mary Palomo and Yolanda Villarreal. All of these sisters were elected to serve on the Educational Board. Mrs. Zamora also is on the Mission Board of 1984.

K. THE LATIN AMERICAN FAMILY OF THE MENNONITE BRETHREN CONFERENCE OF NORTH AMERICA

The Latin American Mennonite Brethren conference came into being because of the vision of the Southern district to evangelize people in the lower Rio Grande Valley of South Texas. Through the years of support by the Southern District, to the time when the support was withdrawn, a faithful group has emerged to form a well-organized conference.

The conference, in 1984, has around 300 members. La Joya has the largest number, La Grulla next, while Donna has the least.

There are however, many more attending each church, so that the worshipping family is between 500 and 600. The church meetings are well attended and Sunday school attendance equals or exceeds the worship services. Some churches even have more attending Sunday night than in the morning. Most churches have something special for children on Wednesday night to attract attendance.

Pharr has had the influx of Winter Texans, some of whom are associate members while they are here.

One great difficulty for proper growth lies in the fact that men, in general, are not willing to join the church and face the ridicule of others. This reluctance is due to a problem unique to the Latin culture — the macho (male) image is very deeply inbred. The Latin culture has coined the word "machismo" which indicates masculine pride or superiority. Paul Castillo, pastor of the La Grulla church, said in 1981 that "Machismo has no room for weakness, and many a Latin male does not like to admit that he needs a Savior. Men believe that church is for women and children but not for them." Some men will not allow any member to attend an evangelical church; others permit the wife and children to go; and a few even believe and attend, but are reluctant to be baptized and make the final break with the world.

When the last support was withdrawn, many were discouraged but others rallied and stuck together. With God's grace they built a conference with the faithful members. By now, in 1984, the members see that in the end it was good for the missions to become churches who look out for themselves.

The ones who have remained faithful, witness to relatives and friends and win some each year. Then some are also won through revival meetings and visitations.

Quoting from *The Christian Leader,* June 29, 1982, "Vitality is particularly evident among the young people, though all age groups are well represented. Many Anglo visitors would be surprised to see the extent to which all groups participate in the congregational life." Among the young there is also love and respect for the older ones, especially grandparents, more so than in Anglo churches. The older folks are greeted by "Hermana" or "Brother" and "Hermana" or "Sister." As a whole, the conference is conservative, still upholding the teachings and examples of the missionaries. This is also due to the fact that many of the pastors have attended Rio Grande Bible Institute and it is strict and conservative.

All of the congregations have struggled with debt. For this reason, the pastors had to earn their own living. The churches gave as much as they were able, but it was not enough. As more and more members enter better paying jobs, the giving has greatly increased.

Together with the tithe of the missionary, there was often enough to pay for Sunday school materials. There are no early records available of just what each church did. In the 1964 report it shows that six churches had spent $521.86 for Sunday school materials and also gave $860.25 to help their pastors. In 1981-1982, the Garciasville, La Grulla, La Joya, Lull, Mission and Pharr Churches gave $24,485 to their pastors. This figure is a large increase, yet it is still little considering the present day cost of living. The report also shows that the same churches spent $30,760.96 on payments on their buildings. The Pharr church, which has the largest debt, receives some help during the time the Winter Texans are there. Only Iglesia de Gracia in Garciasville, Donna, La Joya, Lull and Mission had no debt on their churches in 1984.

The congregations have learned to give and need to learn to win others in the same way, with sacrifice.

Through the years the women in the churches outnumbered the men and also did much of the work. They were elected to serve on the church councils with the men as well as delegates to the conference. They have been the Bible students and prayer warriors in the churches.

More contact with the Spanish churches in California is anticipated. Baltazar Garcia, a Mennonite Brethren pastor from Dinuba, California, was invited to speak at a series of special meetings. Paul Castillo, a native of Mission, now pastors a church in California.

A letter from the District Minister, Arthur Flaming, written May 10, 1966, is still applicable, and it is given here. It is called, "My Observations":

"It seems that the need and the burden and confession of our South Texas churches is the same as it is in 17 churches I have been in this past year — NAMELY; a desperate and great need to go out in visitation! This problem is not unique to South Texas, it is general.

I would like to encourage the pastors in South Texas to offer courses to their people in how to conduct home Bible studies. I feel that they should set definite goals of growth. The pastor will need to lead his people but he must also organize his people, making assignments for visitations.

Records need to be kept in visitation work, together with a follow-up of visitation to Sunday school and church services.

We have a fine group of pastors and their wives in south Texas. It was a joy to fellowship with them, to listen to their problems, to be blessed in their open honesty as they discussed their problems. I was encouraged in my visit to South Texas and feel that God will do a wonderful work there among the people and through our workers."

Great things God has done, yet we look for the time when more men will accept the Lord to build an even greater, stronger conference.

CHAPTER 15

THE PICTURE HISTORY OF LATIN AMERICAN MENNONITE BRETHREN IN TEXAS

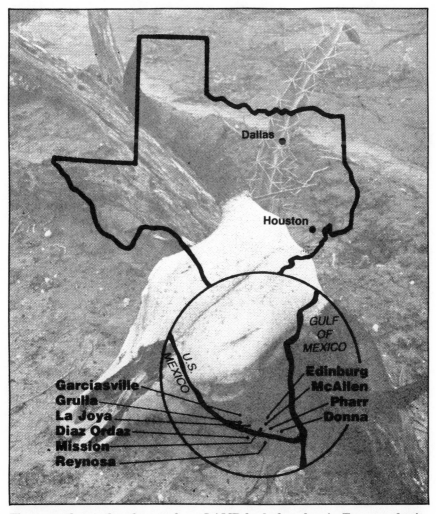

The map shows the places where LAMB had churches in Texas and missions in Mexico in 1984

The First Mennonite Brethren Mission in Texas

A 1931 Chevrolet coupe was used to pull a 9 x 10 trailer house. In this Harry and Sarah Neufeld traveled along the border of Texas from Brownsville to El Paso. They found a field between Mission and Rio Grande City at Los Ebanos.

Welcome: The first congregation in Los Ebanos in 1938.

This was the first rented house in Los Ebanos that was home for Harry and Sarah Neufeld.

This shows the back of the home they built and moved into in 1944. It is on the main street that leads into the village.

Harry, Gordon and Sarah Neufeld in their modern home in Los Ebanos.

This shows the inside of the first meeting place in Los Ebanos where Harry Neufeld conducted services. The verse over the door is John 3:16. This place at first had no windows.

Others came to help build this church. It was dedicated March 29, 1942. A tower was added later as well as a porch and a fence. It served until 1968. It was dismantled in 1969.

This was the baptism of Abelardo Mireles Sr. He was baptized in the Rio Grande River June 5, 1938. This was the first baptism and made a great impression on the villagers.

This is Sarah Neufeld with one of the first Women's Bible Classes on the mission field. This was a special day for the many children who also came. Other missionaries also held Bible class at Los Ebanos.

Harry Neufeld had the first well-trained church choir at Los Ebanos.

The Mennonite Brethren Church at Chihuahua

This was the first church built on the field. Harry Neufeld is standing beside it. It cost $130.00 to build in the village of Chihuahua.

This is the front showing the sign after it was painted. A mesquite grew just in front of it. Harry Neufeld and Eleso Mireles painted it. The sign says, "The Church of the Lord of Mennonite Brethren."

Henry and Ruth Thomas came to this congregation in 1942 with Marlin and Danny. This picture was taken 3 years later at their home in Abram.

This church was built when Henry Thomas was pastor at Chihuahua during 1946. It was dedicated April 28, 1946, but not finished on the inside.

The sign says: Evangelical Church Mennonite Brethren. Services each Sunday at 10:00 AM and 7:00 PM, Wednesdays 7:30 PM. Everybody welcome. Rev. H.F. Thomas, Pastor.

This shows the large mesquite trees and the congregation when Dan Wirsche was pastor. This building was dismantled in 1969 to make the new big church at La Joya. The annex is shown at the left.

This was a Sunday
School group. The girl
next to Henry Thomas
was Marta Espinoza,
the first convert to be
baptized and join the
Chihuahua church.

This is Susie Martin
with the only English
Sunday School class
at Chihuahua.

This is Ruth Thomas
with one of her Bible
classes. This one was
two miles north at
Perezville. She had as
many as six classes a
week.

This house was moved from the D.T. Ediger ranch to Abram and was home to Henry and Ruth until it was enlarged to become a modern home.

Palms and shrubs were planted about on the two-acre plot which remained property of Chihuahua church until it was sold to help build the new big church in La Joya.

This shows the new church in Chihuahua begun Sept. 19, 1984. The ribbon was cut almost a year later. The sign says New Life Temple M.B. Church. Inocencio Garcia is on the porch and Antonio Garcia is on the step. The church is paid for and is planning a Sunday School wing.

The Mennonite Brethren Church in La Grulla

This was the parsonage rebuilt in 1951. Part of it was a little house moved from Chihuahua. The garage served Ruben and Eva Wedel for their services until the church was built.

This was the largest church on the field at the time it was built in March 1949. It was dedicated January 22, 1950, and Sunday School rooms in back were added later and dedicated May 30, 1954. The name on the porch says Mennonite Brethren Church, in Spanish.

Ruben and Eva Wedel and their adopted sons David (standing) and Darold. The Wedels opened the station at La Grulla in 1945 and served until 1956.

This shows a joint baptism of La Grulla and Chihuahua held in Walker Lake in 1952.

The Ruben Wedel family and Yolanda Villarreal who held many Child Evangelism classes in La Grulla and also in El Faro school.

This is the ground breaking service at La Grulla in 1978 for a new tile building. Alvin Neufeld had drawn the plans.

This shows how they put on the roof. It is a view showing the educational wing to the left. Construction began in summer of 1978.

This is a front view of the finished new church at La Grulla.

This shows the interior. It was the dedication service in March of 1979.

The new parsonage was built where the old one stood. It was completed in May 1983.

This is the pastor, José J. and Dina Delgado, with daughter Azucena. They came from California to move into the new parsonage on June 1, 1983.

El Faro School

The Buildings

A ground breaking service took place on a four-acre plot east of Sullivan City north of Los Ebanos. A barrack was bought to begin classes in September of 1948.

The El Faro school building was finished and dedicated February 27, 1949. There were 113 pupils the first year. This is the west side of the tile block building.

The elementary school wall facing south is to the left, built in 1948. The four large classrooms were for the upper grades and high school, built in 1951. The roundtop in the back was the gymnasium and auditorium built in 1953.

El Faro School as seen from the east. The original El Faro School building of 1948 showing the ends of the four class rooms running east and west and the round top north of the rest of the school.

The rented teacherage in Los Ebanos during 1949 used until the new one was ready.

The 1951 teacherage was built a little south of the original school. It has three apartments.

This house and another one were moved to El Faro grounds for teachers and classrooms. The barrack was dismantled and used to build a garage and the teacherage.

Some El Faro Activities

This picture shows
Marinana Wiens and
her Bible class of 4th
graders. Bible was the
first period of the day.
She taught 1956-1969.

Ruth Wiens out east
of the school in a P.E.
class. She was also El
Faro grade principal
1954-1969.

David Fast teaching
5th grade arithmetic.
He taught 1962-1966.

Elaine Schroeder
teaching 6th grade
science. She taught it
also in other grades,
1961-1965.

Daniel Wirsche teach-
ing algebra in grade
9. He taught 1960-
1968.

José Lara teaching
grade 10 typing. He
taught 1963-1965.

Every Christmas El Faro presented a gospel program. Many came to see and hear children and older ones perform in the El Faro auditorium which held hundreds of people.

Field day was another annual event where it was decided who were the best athletes of each grade. The winners received awards. Various physical events took place. It was a great day for all, especially the winners of awards.

Lunch time, a daily event when children lined up before the school store. In later years it was for milk or a hot lunch. The Hot Lunch program was aided by government funds and began in 1965 and ended in 1969.

El Faro had choirs each year. This is the one of 1964. They sang in the various churches.

The Girls' Trio who went to the Southern District Conference. To the right is Ricardo Peña who took the girls to show what El Faro could do.

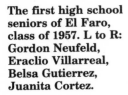

The first high school seniors of El Faro, class of 1957. L to R: Gordon Neufeld, Eraclio Villarreal, Belsa Gutierrez, Juanita Cortez.

El Faro Teachers

Alvina Fast, the first principal 1948-1951.

The first teachers of El Faro, 1948: H.T. Esau, Viola Warkentin, Alvina Fast, Susie Martin.,

Elizabeth Adrian 1951-1961; Susie Martin 1948-1956; Harold Warkentin 1949-1954; Albert Epp 1951-1961. Albert became superintendent 1957-1961.

Latin Americans who taught in El Faro

Olga Guerra
1954-1956

Leonel Saenz
1956-1957

Alpha Guerra
1957-1959

Belsa Gutierrez
1962-1965, 1969

José Lara
1963-1965

Nilda Cantu
1965-1966

El Faro School Superintendents

Raymond Vogt
1955-1957

Albert Epp
1957-1961

Paul Wiebe
1961-1962

Daniel Wirsche
1962-1966

Frank Munoz
1966-1968

El Faro Teachers of 1967-1968

Ruth Wiens, principal, 1954-1969; Elfrieda Buller, 1968-1969; Cathrine Crandall, 1967-1969; Max Bulsterbaum, 1967-1969; Frank Munoz, 1965-1968; Mariana Wiens, 1956-1969; Henry Boese, 1949-1968; Alvina Boese, 1948-1968; Daniel Wirsche, 1962-1968; Elsie Wirsche, 1966-1968; Ofelia Tagle, 1967-1969.

Harry Neufeld is ready to go get children in one of the El Faro busses. They lined up after school to load the children to go home.

Henry Boese was the chief custodian and bus driver for many years at El Faro.

Boards That Operated El Faro

First El Faro School Board, 1948

They are: Ruben Wedel, Harry Neufeld, Henry Thomas and Ricardo Peña. Ricardo stayed on the Board 21 years.

William Neufeld, Raymond Vogt, David Plett, J.R. Bergman, Abe Klassen.

El Faro Board of 1968

Anselmo Salinas, Alfredo Tagle, H.T. Esau, Frank Munoz, Ricardo Peña and Leonel Saenz.

The Premont Station, a Southern District M.B. Mission Work

This little chapel was bought by the Premont M.B. Church in 1946. It was on a 25 ft. lot, very near neighbors who did not like the mission. The Southern District Conference bought it.

The Chapel of the Lord built in 1950 and dedicated on December 26, 1952. The left addition had two Sunday School rooms, which also served as overflow space.

Anna, Kenneth and Henry Esau before their own home on the Premont station, on the mission station on S. East 3rd street.

The group to which
H.T. and Anna Esau
came in Premont.
Ricardo Peña is at the
right near Anna Esau.
This was in the old lit-
tle chapel. An oil well
is showing in the mid-
dle of the picture.

This was the first
Bible school in the
new chapel in 1950.
Alvina Fast is helping
children to line up to
enter classes.

This is a group ready to leave to conduct evangelism classes in homes. They
are Anna Esau, Criselda Garza, Lucinda Quintanilla and Cruz Garza.

The Mennonite Brethren Church at La Joya

This shows the cement block church built on the corner of 1st St. and Garza Ave. in La Joya during 1953. It was dedicated March 7, 1954. Ricardo and Carmen Villarreal Peña were the first workers at this place. The building to the right is the new church which was begun in 1969.

Carmen and Ricardo Peña were married in 1953 and served at La Joya until 1961.

The first day the members of Los Ebanos and Chihuahua all came to La Joya was May 12, 1968 for a Mothers' Day program. The church was full. This is the first church built at La Joya in 1953.

This is the new church showing Alfredo and Ofelia Tagle standing at the south end of the sanctuary. The east entrance is at the end of the walkway. This church was dedicated October 25, 1970, at 3 PM. The Administrative Committee and the pastor, Alfredo Tagle, entered this east door.

Pictured on the stage are left to right: Ruben Wedel, Ricardo Peña, Frank Munoz, Alfred Tagle behind the pulpit, Alvin Neufeld, choir members and Wesley Wirsche, chairman of the Administrative Committee.

The La Joya Mennonite Brethren church as seen from the west. The entrance under the porch enters the educational wing and the walk leads to the foyer of the sanctuary.

The parsonage at Los Ebanos built by Harry Neufeld served the Alfred Tagle family until they moved into their own home. The children are Benjamine, Ruth, Moises, and Elizabeth holding a doll. This shows the house from the street in Los Ebanos.

Daniel and Elsie Wirsche live on the church yard in their own mobile home. They were installed as pastor January 20, 1985.

The Mennonite Brethren Church at Lull (Edinburg)

Alvin and Ruth Neufeld with Phillip and Phoebe parked beside this Baptist church in Lull in 1951-1952. They began to build their own home in 1952 for services.

The church was built in 1953. It shows the loudspeaker on the tower. To the right of the church, built on Rodriguez and Furntes, is the parsonage before there were trees.

This shows the church after the hurricane of 1967 damaged the tower and the roof. At the far left you see the ice plant which gives the name of La Hielera to this village.

This shows the new Sunday School addition that was added to the Lull church in spring of 1961. A group of children are playing during Bible school. Valentina Flores was their teacher.

This shows the bookends, figurines and plaques the Lull children made in 1963. Anna Esau designed them.

The Lull church was redecorated and bricked while Anselmo Salinas was pastor during the late seventies. The sign is in English, "Lull Mennonite Brethren Church," also in Spanish saying that Crispin Diaz is the pastor.

Crispin and Angela Diaz. He was installed as pastor on October 24, 1982.

The Casita-Garciasville Church

This is the chapel that was built in Casita and dedicated Nov. 29, 1953. It was moved by Albert Epp to a good-sized plot in Garciasville. The porch was added by Inocencio Garcia and the sign was put up while Pedro Durik was pastor.

Early in 1972 a new roof was put on and the Sunday School wing was enlarged. In Feb. 1973 new windows were installed and the next year the Corn and Cordell workers finished the inside.

This picture shows a group on a Sunday in 1974. In 1975 a group led by Albert Epp came to finish the educational wing.

In spring of 1976 the Oklahoma folks came with Albert Epp and put on the south entrance wing with new glass doors to the east. The Epps returned for the dedication August 1, 1976. The right wing is the social hall and has rooms for Sunday School classes. This picture was taken on dedication day.

This shows the last addition to the north giving three Sunday School rooms. Dan Stobbe and Edd Vogt from Corn, Oklahoma came to supervise and build this part of the church. The church has no debt.

This shows Jessie Guerra conducting meetings out on the Casita village plaza night after night.

This shows the place of union services in Rio Grande City at the home of Roberto Sandoval. The chairs came from El Faro. Paulino Bernal, a converted dance band director, gave his story that night.

This shows Minnie Saenz bringing in children for Vacation Bible School in Garciasville.

In 1957 the Albert Epps moved a small house from El Faro to Garciasville and rebuilt it. This has been the parsonage all the years.

Carlos and Emma Roman came from Reynosa to live in the parsonage at Garciasville. The children are Carlos Armando, Jessica and Mario. Carlos Roman was installed as pastor October 23, 1982.

The Church at Mission

This is the first church built at Chihuahua. It was moved to the lots on Perez Street in Mission by Inocencio Garcia, the first missionary to Mission.

This shows Inocencio Garcia and a group from Mission at the ground breaking service on Perez Street late in 1956 in preparation to build a new church.

This shows the end of the church in Mission on Perez St.

Victor and Elizabeth Fast came to build the new, much larger church in 1957 and 1958.

The new church built on Perez St. served until 1972 when Ricardo Peña bought lots on Holland Avenue across the street from a school. This church was moved and the steeple removed and set down facing north as it had on Perez Street.

The church from Perez St. is the part to the right. The part to the left is the
new social hall, kitchen and Sunday School rooms. This picture was taken
before the Christmas freeze of 1983 that killed the big tree. The sign says
Evangelical Church, Mennonite Brethren, 300 Holland Ave. The entire
building was covered with white bricks.

John and Becky
Neufeld Wall. They
began their service in
the Mission church on
November 8, 1981.

The McAllen-Pharr Church

This shows the rented house with a steeple and sign added by Alvin Neufeld in 1964. It was on 1718 Maple Street in McAllen. The sign says "Open Bible Church."

Alvin and Ruth Neufeld, pastor and Ruben and Eva Wedel, assistant pastor in McAllen. This shows the front of the house.

Mennonite Brethren Bible Church, Pharr

The McAllen group moved into this building on W. 823 FM 495 in March 1969. The first bilingual service was held September 9, 1973, with Tim Kliewer as pastor.

Tim was ordained March 10, 1974. Alvin Neufeld welcomes Tim and Myrna as the pastor of the English congregation. Alvin continued to serve the Spanish group.

This church on 413 N. Sugar Road was bought Jan. 1, 1975, and named Mennonite Brethren Bible Church. The flat roof was the educational wing and social hall. It is a double walled brick structure.

The present Pharr Mennonite Brethren Church as seen from the southeast. It is on Sugar Road and the big tree is a pecan. The double door forms the east entrance. The new hip roof was built by John Yoder in 1981.

This shows the asphalt parking lot and the west entrance under the porch. Two date palms survived the big frost.

Present Workers at Mennonite Brethren Church at Pharr.

Tom and Linda Haughey with Dawn
came to serve in 1984. He is pastor
and preaches in English.

Alvin and Ruth Neufeld have been
with the work since its beginning in
McAllen. He looks after the Spanish
services.

Gabriel and Lupita Ledesma are
helpers in the Spanish work. The
baby is little Aaron.

The Mennonite Brethren Church at Donna

This shows the brick church that M.C. Ehlert began in Donna. Enrique and Julia Galvan were in charge of the church owned by the Rio Grande Bible Institute when it was sold to LAMB Conference. The local congregation payed for it and the Galvans stayed at the church.

This shows Mr. and Mrs. Rafael Plazola before the church which had been painted since it was bought in 1966.

Enrique Galvan added a baptistry to the church. He used it in 1967. There were also two small rooms. In 1984 the church extended the Sunday School space.

For three years Henry and Anna Esau went to Donna in summer to conduct Bible school. The picture shows a craft class taught out under a big tree. The children loved to paint plaques.

This shows the Rafael Plazolas standing in front of the parsonage which is on the same yard with the church. They were RGBI students who lived in Donna while attending school during 1972.

Herculano and Matilda Cornejo took charge of the group and it again began to grow. He was installed as pastor in May of 1981.

Anglo Missionaries Accepted and Sent By
Mennonite Brethren Southern District Conference

Left to right: Ruben and Eva Wedel, La Grulla, 1945-1956; Harry and Sarah Neufeld at Los Ebanos, 1937-1957; Henry and Anna Esau at Premont, 1948-1960; Henry and Ruth Thomas at Chihuahua, 1942-1960; Ricardo Peña, Havana, Premont, Casita and La Joya, 1947-1960. Harold and Rosena Warkentin served at Havana and Casita 1949-1954.

Albert and Emily Epp family in 1976. They were at Garciasville 1951-1961.

John and Daphyn Savoia and family taken the last years at La Grulla. They served at Casita and La Grulla 1954-1959.

Not pictured were Eugene and Lillian Janzen at Los Ebanos, 1958-1960 and Ricardo and Grace Zapata at Los Ebanos and Casita, 1951-1954.

The Pastors and Their Churches That
Formed LAMB Conference in South Texas in 1963.

The Los Ebanos con-
gregation before their
church as it looked in
1963. The sign says
The Church of the
Lord. This church was
dedicated March 29,
1942.

José Lara was pastor
at Los Ebanos in 1963.
José and Graciela
both came from
Mexico but were edu-
cated in America. He
taught in El Faro. The
boys are Jorge and
Jaime.

The Chihuahua
Church and congrega-
tion in 1963. This
church was built by
Henry Thomas and
dedicated April 27,
1946.

Daniel and Elsie
Wirsche and their
sons, Stanley, Wesley,
Peter and Donald,
were in charge of the
Chihuahua Church in
1963. They had
worked in Colombia
and In Mexico.

Ruben Wedel held ser-
vices in the garage
until the church could
be built. The La
Grulla church was the
largest one on the
field. It was built in
March of 1949 and
finished and dedi-
cated in January 22,
1950.

During the time the
LAMB Conference
was organized, Al-
fredo and Ofelia Tagle
lived at La Grulla. The
children are Benja-
min, Elizabeth, Ruth
and Moises.

The La Joya Church
was built of cement
blocks from money
sent as a gift. Ricardo
and Carmen Peña
opened this field. This
church was dedicated
March 7, 1954.

Daniel and Geneva
Kime were in charge
of La Joya when the
LAMB Conference
began to operate. The
children are Kennert,
Danny and Alane.

The chapel was first
built in Casita and
moved to Garciasville
by Albert Epp. In-
ocencio Garcia built
the front porch. Al-
fredo Tagle, standing
at the left, was pastor
during 1963 but lived
in the La Grulla par-
sonage.

The church at Lull (Edinburg) was built by Alvin Neufeld in 1953. The part to the left is the educational wing. The Lull station did not belong to the Southern District Conference, but is a part of LAMB now.

In 1963 Inocencio Garcia became pastor at Lull. Left to right, the first three are Anselmo and Lucia Salinas, Lydia, Maria and Lucia. Amelia and Inocencio are at the right.

The Mission M.B. Church was opened by Inocencio Garcia. This church was built in 1957-1958. It was dedicated in 1959. By 1963 Ricardo and Carmen Peña were in charge. The children are Carlos, Freddy, Dina, Ricky, Becky and David.

The Alvin Neufeld family in 1963 when they left Lull to move to McAllen. They are Phoebe, Philip, Ruth, Alvin, Naomi Jean, Paul, Stanley and Becky. The work in McAllen did not develop but it led to a church in Pharr.

Frank and Mary Jean Munoz and their children in 1963. They are Jonathan, David and Debra. The Munoz family went to live and work at La Grulla 1963-1969.

The Administrative Board of the new LAMB Conference. They are Alfredo Tagle, Inocencio Garcia, Alvin Neufeld, Federico Garcia, Antonio Garcia and Daniel Wirsche. Inocencio was chosen chairman, therefore, became the first conference moderator.

The LAMB Conference

Alfredo and Olfelia Tagle of Los Ebanos. In 1960 he was chosen to be the chairman of the Provisional Administrative Committee that brought about the LAMB Conference.

Inocencio Garcia and Amelia. LAMB chairman 1963-1969.

Inocencio Garcia and Oralia, pastor of Garciasville and La Joya.

Jonas Ybarra was elected chairman of LAMB Administrative Committee on Nov. 18, 1966 and served until April 3, 1967 when he became vice chairman. Inocencio Garcia served as chairman.

Enrique Galvan was elected Nov. 27, 1967 and served until June when he moved away. Inocencio Garcia finished the year. (Picture of Galvan is in the section on the Donna church.)

Rolando Mireles has served as chairman of LAMB Administrative Board since November, 1979. He and Lucila are from the La Grulla church.

Wesley and Zita Wirsche are from the La Joya church. He has been LAMB Administrative Chairman from 1969 to 1979 when he became secretary.

The Administrative Committee elected 1984

Left to right: Alfredo Tagle (Lull); Wesley Wirsche (La Joya), secretary; Herculano Cornejo (Donna); Rudolfo Peña (Mission); Kenneth Esau (Pharr), treasurer; Rolando Mireles (La Grulla), chairman.

LAMB Board of Trustees

Left to right: José Delgado (La Grulla); Rudulfo Peña (Mission); Alvin Neufeld (Pharr), treasurer; Ramon Flores (Lull); Roberto Zamora (Mission), secretary; John Wall (Mission) chairman.

LAMB Board of Education of 1984

Left to right: Alvin Neufeld, chairman; Mrs. Gregoria Guerra, secretary; Mrs. Idalia Chapa; Miss Elizabet Tagle; Miss Yolanda Villearreal and Maria Palomo, treasurer (not pictured).

LAMB Board of Missions, left to right: José Delgado, La Grulla (chairman); Crispin Diaz, Lull: Ricardo Peña; Mrs. Angelica Zamora, Mission (secretary). Back row: John Wall, Mission (treasurer) and Ramon Flores.

LAMB CYF Committee of 1984: Moises Tagle, La Grulla (sponsor); Elizabet Tagle, Lull (secretary); Mirta Cantu, La Grulla (chairperson); Mary Malonado, Mission; Clay Canchez, La Joya (treasurer) not pictured.

La Fuente Viva, a LAMB Radio program. This shows Alvin Neufeld in his own studio preparing the tapes for La Fuente Viva (The Living Fountain). It began in 1966 and ceased in 1977. The LAMB churches paid for the program. Alfredo Tagle was the first conference-elected radio pastor.

A Bible Conference in 1955 held at El Faro. Hundreds came at that time and heard the gospel. There were sessions for all ages.

On the stage are Linda Fast, Ruben Wedel and Eleanor Vogt at the piano. This was a meeting at El Faro in 1951.

The LAMB Youth, now called CYF (Christian Youth Fellowship) meets monthly and has its own conference. Since 1969 the CYF is a standing committee of the LAMB Conference.

Women's LAMB Conference that met at Garciasville. The picture shows some of them being served a meal after the conference session. These represent the women of the various churches. They were organized as a conference in spring of 1961. They have two conferences a year.

The first Men's Breakfast met at Garciasville May 28, 1976. Inocencio Garcia became the first president. They seek to win men and collect money for various causes. The picture was taken at La Grulla. The men meet one Sunday morning a month.

LAMB Mission Work in Mexico

This shows the first mission work done by any member of the mission churches in Texas. Alfredo Villearreal from the Los Ebanos church is seen standing at the right. He crossed the Rio Grande in a boat to give the gospel to his relatives in and around San Miguel now Dias Ordaz. Harry and Sarah Neufeld with some guests were visiting Alfredo's services under a portal in 1950.

This shows the Rio Grande River and the hand-drawn ferryboat landing in Los Ebanos. Just across the river is Diaz Ordaz and the church started by Alfredo Villearreal and kept going by German Contreras.

The Diaz Ordaz Mennonite Brethren Church,
a Mission of LAMB

The town of Diaz
Ordaz.

The front of the M.B.
church built by Al-
fredo Villearreal and
German Contreras.
The work was begun
in 1954.

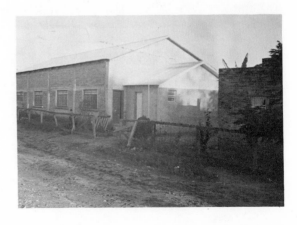

The back of the
church showing class-
rooms.

The parsonage built of cement blocks has served all through the years.

The German Contreras family. Bertha holds the youngest, Neftal. Eunice the second oldest is not pictured. The rest are Jonatan, David, Josue, Laura, Azael and Rebeca.

LAMB Work in Reynosa

Carlos and Emma de Leon Roman came to Reynosa with Carlos Armando in 1977. They lived and worked from a house. In 1982 40 to 50 persons came to the services.

This is the building that was bought in 1982. It is located five miles down on Matamoros Road in Colonia Juarez. The door to the right enters the chapel and the part to the left is the parsonage. The addition was begun in 1983. It is built so a second story can be added later.

The sign on the mission in Reynosa says: Evangelical Church "Emmanuel" Mennonite Brethren "Enter to worship and leave to serve".

A group from the Reynosa mission church.

The pastor, Miguel de Leon, who came in 1982. The three are baptism candidates who were instructed and baptized by the pastor.

The workers at Reynosa church are left to right: the pastor, Miguel de Leon; Ricardo Peña, and just behind them are Yolanda Villearreal, her sister, Carmen Peña, hidden behind Ricardo, and Dina Medina, a daughter of the Peña's. The rest are people from the church.

Carmen Peña and her Sunday School class.

Agripina, from the church, and her class.

LAMB's New Work at Magueyes

This is the place where Yolanda Villearreal and Inez Cabrera went to conduct Child Evangelism classes on the second floor in 1980. In 1984 a group of believers met in another building just behind this one in Magueyes.

A home in the village of Piño Suarez a mile from Magueyes showing the Sierra Madre mountains in the background. The peak is called Pico de Pilon by the people and the river is Rio de Pilon. This shows the palm thatched roofs of the pole huts. The ox cart is ready to go.

People live near the river to get water. Ricardo Peña is seen shaving at the river.

Water has to be carried on a shoulder yoke. This picture shows Inez Cabrera going to the river for water.

This shows the village oxen team going to work.

This is a front view of a home decorated with pots and plants. The people are Inez Cabrera from Mission and her mother with Ricardo Peña, a member of the LAMB Mission Board.

The Cabrera family built this cement block house for workers to live in while serving the group at Magueyes. The mountains are seen looking southwest. Lots have been donated for a future church building, but the title needs to be cleared.

EVENTS THAT OCCURRED DURING 1985-1987 IN THE LAMB CHURCHES

The Donna M.B. Church built a cement block addition of 44'x16' to their chapel. This gives them rooms for their Sunday School classes. The new white building is in the back and extends out toward the east.

The La Grulla M.B. Church lost its pastor, José Delgado, who left to serve as chaplain in the armed forces. Rolando Mireles and Aneceto Zarate fill the pulpit unless others can be found.

The Mission M.B. Church changed pastors. John and Becky Wall left August 15, 1985. They entered Mennonite Brethren Biblical Seminary in Fresno, California in January, 1986. Later they accepted a call to the Spanish M.B. Church at Dinuba. Alfredo and Ofelia Tagle were installed as the new workers at Mission on March 2, 1986.

The Pharr M.B. Bible Church has seen major changes. Alvin Neufeld, the assistant pastor, laid down the Spanish preaching work in spring of 1986 and Gabriel Ledesma and Lupe left in September of 1986. Since then Tom Haughey preaches in English and then in Spanish. February 1, 1987 Simon and Silvia Perez were ordained at Pharr. The Perez's have the only bilingual radio program of Zapoteco and Spanish in the Oaxaca province in Mexico. The programs are aired at 7:00 a.m. and at 2:00 p.m. on Sundays.

The La Joya Church refinished their dark pews. They are beautiful.

La Iglesia de Gracia at Garciasville. The pastor, Carlos Roman and family, moved to Rio Grande City where he took a job. He still serves the church.

Youth of LAMB: Some 45 young people of the LAMB churches worked hard to raise money to attend Glorieta '87, quadrennial U.S. Conference Youth Convention in March. The following adults went with them: Rolando and Lucila Mireles, Aneceto and Imelda Zarate from La Grulla; Wesley and Zita Wirsche, Domingo and Rosela Villearreal from La Joya; Moisés and Elizabeth Tagle, Angel Cabrera, Roldolfo and Adella Peña and Esperanza Palomo from Mission.

183

THE LAMB MISSION CHURCHES IN MEXICO

Reynosa LAMB Mission Church: Ricardo and Carmen Peña still go to to help each Sunday in Reynosa. The churches had their first missionary conference at Reynosa. People came from Dias Ordaz and Magueyes as well as representatives from the churches in Texas. It was a day of rejoicing for these believers to meet and have part in the program.

Magueyes LAMB Mission Church: In 1980 Yolanda Villearreal and Inez Cabrera began working with children in Magueyes. Inez has been going most weekends to help in the group that has been saved. At the conference of 1986 Angel Cabrera and his sister Inez, Mrs. Angelica Zamora and Yolanda Villearreal pledged themselves to pay for a lot and two buildings in a good location in Magueyes. It will take four years to pay for it. Both of the buildings need windows and walls to form rooms. The group there is willing to do what they can to pay for the improvements.

Dias Ordaz LAMB Mission Church: The Dias Ordaz Church has a new pastor since 1986. The picture shows the Maurilio Loya family with five children. They are Pastor Maurilio and his wife Elvia and the children, Elia Ruth (9) the only daughter and four boys – Obed Azael (7), twins Israel Maurilio and Ismael Mauricio (5) and Jairo Eliel (2). (Feb. 1987) The Loyas met in Bible School Instituto Practico Ebenezar at Hermosillo, Senora, Mexico. They have served other churches for ten years and now they have the conviction the Lord led them to the Mennonite Brethren. They have repaired the parsonage and made improvements in the church.

The new pastor who came in August 1986 is Jorge de Leon. He is a brother to the pastor at Reynosa and also has been in Seminario Biblico. He is married and has two small children. His wife is Rosita and the children are Sandra and Jorge Jr. who is a baby.

The German Contreras Family all grew up in Dias Ordaz. Standing are: Rebeca, Jonatan, David, Laura, Josue, Asael and Eunice. Seated: Neftal, the youngest and German and Bertha, the parents. These served for many years.

CHAPTER BACKGROUND NOTES

PREFACE
Reports from the Foreign Mission Board, Mennonite Brethren Conference
Information from the Office of the District Minister, Hillsboro, Kansas

CHAPTER I; THE LOWER RIO GRANDE VALLEY OF TEXAS
Eight Years Among Latin Americans, Harry Neufeld.
Experiences of H.T. Esau in the school.
"The Family in the Valley," Wally Kroeker, *The Christian Leader,* June 29, 1982.
Personal contact with the people from Mexico and with Pan American students.
Personal knowledge of the Valley, Hurricane Beulah, Falcon Dam as well as a knowledge of the people and their language.
Radio and TV reports.
The Reader's Digest Great Encyclopedic Dictionary.
Term paper by Rafaela Villalon about superstition in the Valley.
Trees of North America, C. Frank Brockman.

CHAPTER II; EARLY EVENTS THAT LED TO THE OPENING OF THE FIELD IN SOUTH TEXAS
Charter and information of John 3:16 Frontier Mission.
Eight Years Among Latin Americans, Harry Neufeld.
Information sent by Sarah Neufeld about the life and work of Harry Neufeld.
Report by Mrs. Henry Andres about the early history and the mission work of P.E. Penner.

CHAPTER III; LOS EBANOS, THE FIRST MENNONITE BRETHREN MISSION ALONG THE RIO GRANDE
Education Board minutes about the Laras.
Eight Years Among Latin Americans, Neufeld.
Information received from Tim Kliewer, Ricardo Peña, and Sarah Neufeld.
Interviews with the Neufelds, Alfredo and Ofelia Tagle and Inocencio Garcia.
Letter from Harry Neufeld, January 8, 1941.
Personal knowledge about the Canosa and the Ortiz.

CHAPTER IV; THE MENNONITE BRETHREN MISSION AT CHIHUAHUA
Eight Years Among Latin Americans, Neufeld.
El Faro annual *GLEAM,* 1968.
Information from and interviews with Sarah Neufeld, Inocencio Garcia, Henry and Susie Martin Thomas, Ricardo Peña, and Daniel and Elsie Wirsche.
Personal knowledge gained through visits.

CHAPTER V; THE MENNONITE BRETHREN CHURCH AT LA GRULLA

Christian Leader, clippings in an album of Ruben Wedel.

Conversion experiences as told by Yolanda Villarreal and Carmen Peña.

History of the La Grulla MB Church, compiled by Rolando Mireles and others.

Information received from many, including Sarah Neufeld, Roland Mireles, Alfredo and Ofelia Tagle, Frank Munoz, Jose J. Delgado, Ruben and Eva Wedel, Yolanda Villarreal, and Inocencio Garcia.

Personal knowledge of the conditions at La Grulla.

CHAPTER VI; THE EL FARO SCHOOL

Education Board minutes, 1965, kept by H.T. Esau.

"El Faro" papers all carried news about the school.

GLEAM, 1951, 1957, 1964, 1966, 1968, all provide information about El Faro, the churches and the mission work.

Information from Ricardo Peña, Frank Munoz, and H.T. Esau, one of the first teachers. Information from the teachers and school records.

Teachers Who Served at El Faro
    Ten or More Years:
Ruth and Mariana Wiens
Albert Epps
Miss Adrian
    Five or More Years:
Henry and Susie Martin Thomas
Harold Warkentin
Daniel and Elsie Wirsche
Eleanor Vogt
David Fast
    Less than Five Years:
Belsa Gutierrez
Ray Vogt
Elaine Schroeder
Connie Savoia
Geneva Kime
Olga Guerra
Jose Lara
Ruth Steward
Frank Munoz
Wilma Smith
Frieda Buller
Tim and Myrna Kliewer
Nilda Cantu
Max Bulsterbaum
Catherine Crandall
Henry T. Esau
Grace Unruh
Leonel Saenz
Alpha Guerra
Dan Petker
Paul and Donna Beth Wiebe
Anna Enns

Margery Erlandson
Yolanda Villarreal
Annie Dyck
Alfredo and Ofelia Tagle
Henry Boese
Zita Wirsche

Personal knowledge of that time, the school, and the school curriculum.

CHAPTER VII; THE MENNONITE BRETHREN MISSION AT PREMONT, TEXAS
"El Faro" newsletter of January, 1953 tells of the dedication at Premont.
GLEAM, 1951, a history of the MB Latin American Gospel Mission.
Personal knowledge, recollection and diary notes from twelve years of work in the area.

CHAPTER VIII; THE CHURCH AT LA JOYA
A brief history of the church by Ricardo Peña.
Conference records and personal report by Alfredo Tagle about evangelistic work at La Joya.
Information from and interviews with Sarah Neufeld, Ricardo and Carmen Peña, Alfredo Tagle, Daniel Kime, Yolanda Villarreal, and Inocencio Garcia.
Information from Wesley Wirsche about the dedication.
Minutes of the Administration Committee.
Personal information from Alfredo Tagle and Yolanda Villarreal on the merging of the La Joya, Los Ebanos and Chihuahua churches.

CHAPTER IX; THE LULL (EDINBURG) MENNONITE BRETHREN CHURCH
Conversion experience as told by Ramon Flores.
Information from Alvin Neufeld, H.T. Esau, Inocencio Garcia and Crispin Diaz about the work among the children; and from Angela Diaz about the work among the women; and from Ruth Neufeld about the work among the sick.
Knowledge of the various workers because of twelve years of work at Lull.

CHAPTER X; THE MENNONITE BRETHREN CHURCH AT CASITA AND GARCIASVILLE
Description about Casita from Ricardo Peña.
Description of the chapel by John Savoia.
El Faro *GLEAM*.
Information from and interviews with Harry Neufeld, Sarah Neufeld, Ricardo Peña, Albert Epp and Inocencio Garcia.
Information from the members of the circle and personal knowledge of the women's work.
Information from the diary of H.T. Esau.
Report by Sarah Neufeld in the El Faro paper.
Writings of Zapata, Savoia and others.

CHAPTER XI; MB MISSION WORK IN MISSION
Information from and interviews with Inocencio Garcia, Ricardo and Carmen

Peña, Mrs. Crispin Diaz, John and Becky Wall and Angela Diaz provided good background for the various aspects of the work at Mission.
Ramon Flores provided information about Warren W. Coles, Mission.
John and Becky Wall confirmed the story about their deacons and also gave information about themselves as well as about Arthur and Helen Dalke.

CHAPTER XII; THE PHARR MENNONITE BRETHREN CHURCH

Alvin and Ruth Neufeld provided information about the work at Pharr and about their family.
Ben H. Wedel reported about his jail ministry.
Information about Tom and Linda Haughey, and Kenneth L. Esau was gleaned by attendance at church.
Information provided by Ben and Frances Wedel, Simon and Silvia Perez, Concepcion Diaz, Ruben and Eva Wedel, and the Alfred Quirings.
Information from Tim Kliewer describing his call and service.
Literature from the Children's Haven and several visits to the orphanage.
Personal knowledge of the dedication and ordination of Tim Kliewer, and of the Kliewer family.
Personal knowledge about McAllen and Pharr.
Reports from TV and radio.

CHAPTER XIII; THE MENNONITE BRETHREN CHURCH AT DONNA

Administrative Committee minutes, 1966, 1969, 1974, kept by Alvin Neufeld.
Information from Alvin Neufeld, Ofelia Tagle and students of RGBI about the work at Donna.
Letter from Ramiro Leal.
Personal acquaintance with and information from Enrique Galvan, Simon Rada and Herculano Cornejo.

CHAPTER XIV; THE LATIN AMERICAN MENNONITE BRETHREN CONFERENCE IN TEXAS

Administrative Committee Minutes, Feb. 4, 1960; March 9, 1963; 1967; Oct. 12, 1969.
Education Board Minutes, 1972.
Conference Reports, March, 1960; January, 1964; November, 1966; October, 1967; 1969; 1970; 1972; 1977.
"The Family in the Valley," *The Christian Leader,* Wally Kroeker, June 19, 1982.
Information obtained from numerous people, including John Wall, Wesley Wirsche, Alvin Neufeld, Sarah Neufeld, Inocencio Garcia, Ruth Thomas, Altagracia Villarreal.
Minutes of the Latin American MB Conference, January 8, 1960; January 25, 1960; and February 4, 1960.
Personal knowledge of the work, including the worker retreats, the transfer from the Southern District to the Foreign Mission work, the first Women's Conference, 1961, and the work of the Education Board.
Letter from Arthur Flaming, Conference Minister of Southern District, May 10, 1966.
The Leaders of the LAMB Conference provided helpful information about themselves and the work.

CHAPTER XV; A PICTORIAL HISTORY OF THE LAMB CHURCHES AND WORKERS

Pictures and information received from the following sources:

H.T. Esau collection

El Faro annual of 1968, a special picture edition for El Faro's 15th Anniversary.

Education Board, especially Alvin Neufeld.

Inocencio Garcia

Sarah Neufeld

Rolando Mireles, especially pictures of La Grulla, and the various boards, pastors.

Henry and Susie Thomas

Ricardo Peña, pictures of the LAMB mission work in Mexico

John Wall

Daniel and Wesley Wirsche sent pictures of La Joya

Jonas Ybarra

The Christian Leader provided the map from the June 29, 1982 issue

CHAPTER XV; PICTURE HISTORY OF THE LAMB CHURCHES AND WORKERS

Pictures and information taken from or given from the following sources:

H.T. Esau collection of pictures and slides

El Faro annual of 1968, Special picture edition of 15th anniversary of El Faro, 1963-1964.

Educational Board especially Alvin Neufeld gave pictures and slides

Inocencio Garcia gave pictures and information

Mrs. Sarah Neufeld sent pictures and information

Rolando Mireles gave pictures of La Grulla, various boards and pastors

Henry and Susie Thomas sent pictures and information

Ricarda Peña sent pictures of LAMB mission work in Mexico

John Wall gave pictures of Mission

Daniel and Wesley Wirsche sent pictures of La Joya

Jonas Ybarra gave picture of himself

Map from *The Christian Leader,* June 29, 1982